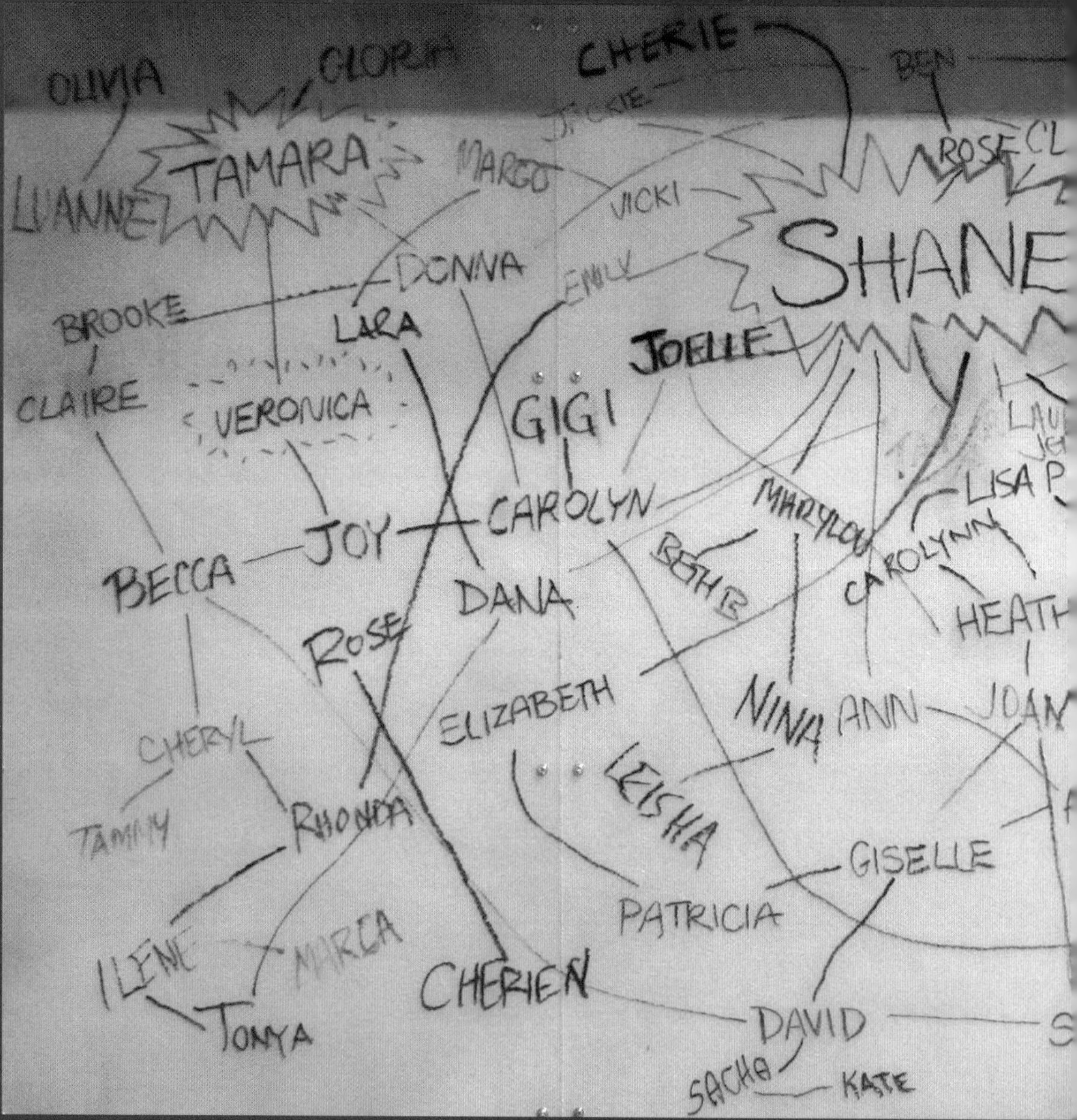
OLIVIA
GLORIA
CHERIE
BEN
JACKIE
TAMARA
MARGO
ROSE
LUANNE
VICKI
SHANE
DONNA
EMILY
BROOKE
LARA
JOELLE
CLAIRE
VERONICA
GIGI
LISA P.
CAROLYN
JOY
MARYLOU
BECCA
BETH B
CAROLYNN
DANA
ROSE
ELIZABETH
NINA
ANN
CHERYL
LEISHA
TAMMY
RHONDA
GISELLE
PATRICIA
ILENE
MARCA
CHERIEN
TONYA
DAVID
SACHA
KATE

AMY — TIM — LARA — DANA — EVE — ERICA
FRANCIS — SARAH
JENNY
ALICE
2MEN — AIESHA
BETTE
ROBIN
CINDY — ROBERTA
TINA
HOPE
CANDACE
LISA
SUNNY
MARINA — VALERIE
KATHRYN
JESSIE
ALINE
HELENA
GWEN
CLAIBURN — JEAN
CYND
MELANIE
SALLEE
LOUISE
HELEN
LAUREN
FRANCESCA
ARLENE
DELANA
REBECCA
ANDREA — ELIZABETH
KEVIN — YOLANDA
AMY
LEAH
LYNN
EY — DANIELLE
AMELE
JOLIE
TROY
DEBBIE

Welcome to the L

word
Our Planet

Kera Bolonik
Introduction by Ilene Chaiken

A Fireside Book
Published by Simon & Schuster
New York   London   Toronto   Sydney

Fireside
Rockefeller Center
1230 Avenue of the Americas
New York, NY 10020

FIRESIDE and colophon are registered trademarks of Simon & Schuster, Inc.

EMMY® is a registered trademark of the Academy of Television Arts and Sciences.
GOLDEN GLOBE® is a registered trademark and service mark of the
Hollywood Foreign Press Association.

For information regarding special discounts for bulk purchases, please contact
Simon & Schuster Special Sales at 1-800-456-6798 or business@simonandschuster.com.

Designed by Charles Kreloff

Manufactured in the United States of America

10   9   8   7   6   5   4   3

ISBN-13: 978-0-7432-9133-0
ISBN-10:   0-7432-9133-6

Contents

Introduction by Ilene Chaiken, Executive Producer/Creator ix

Looking at the Big Picture (on the Small Screen):
How *The L Word* Is Changing the World 1

L Is for Los Angelenas (and a Few Los Angelenos) 5

Landing on Earth...lings: The Pilot 74

Season One: Episode Guide 85

L Is for Lovefaking: Demystifying the Sex Scene 133

L Is for Looks: The L Wardrobe 140

Season Two: Episode Guide 155

Looking Behind the Curtain: The L Crew 211

A Look at Season Three 238

Acknowledgments 242

Introduction
by Ilene Chaiken

There is an experience shared by so many lesbians and gay men to whom I've spoken. They love movies and television, and they savor the great stories—stories of adventure, courage, struggle, triumph, redemption, love . . . Ah, but when they get to the "love" part, there has always been a little internal maneuver they've had to carry out. They transpose. Usually unconsciously and with fairly little effort, nonetheless they have, throughout their lives, translated and transposed and reorganized hundreds of stories of heterosexual love to their own homosexual experience, substituting their fantasies and their obstacles, their objects of desire, themselves for a person of the opposite gender. Take that swooning love scene in *A Place in the Sun*—so moving, so memorable, so life-altering for me. Of course, it wasn't the Elizabeth Taylor character to whom I related; not for even a moment did I want to kiss Montgomery Clift, beautiful and effeminate as he was. I wanted to *be* Montgomery Clift, kissing Elizabeth Taylor. And when Lauren Bacall put the moves on Humphrey Bogart in *To Have and Have Not*—well, it was never that much of a stretch, was it?—to morph Lauren Bacall into a sexy butch top seducing some equally suave but smitten dyke. Still, gay people's stories were largely unrepresented in the popular culture, especially the stories of their emotional and romantic lives. Even as gay people have been responsible for creating or enriching much of that culture, they've endured and accepted their own invisibility. Until recently, they haven't really had a choice.

"Queer as Folk, Will & Grace, Queer Eye for the Straight Guy—none of those shows was yet on the air."

When I first proposed to Showtime the notion to do an hourlong, prime-time weekly ensemble drama about lesbians, the proposition was fairly audacious. *Queer as Folk, Will & Grace, Queer Eye for the Straight Guy*—none of those shows was yet on the air. To my knowledge, the only television show ever to feature a lesbian series regular was a little-known and short-lived Aaron Spelling drama from the mid-1980s—*HeartBeat*—about a women's ob-gyn collective in Los Angeles. (I know; but let's not go into the reasons why the show never found an audience.) As it happens, I was the head of development for Aaron Spelling at the time and integrally involved in the development of that show. The real-life clinic that served as the inspiration for *HeartBeat* was run by several doctors who were lesbians. The only lesbian character

"What neither Showtime nor I knew was that the audience for our 'little lesbian show' would comprise such a large, diverse, and passionately engaged assortment of people."

in the series, however, was a nurse practitioner in a long-term committed relationship with a social worker who had a child from a heterosexual marriage. When Gail Strickland was cast, she felt that she needed to research details about her character—not the nurse practitioner details, the lesbian details. She asked if she could come to my house and hang out with my partner and me in order to get a sense of what a real lesbian relationship looked and acted like. That's how invisible lesbians were back then. Some fifteen years after *HeartBeat* had come and gone—and after the significant but fleeting advent of Ellen DeGeneres in her first foray as an out lesbian on *Ellen*—lesbians were still invisible. Only after the gay boys had three high-visibility prime-time hits on the air did the lesbian show finally see the light of day.

I never even pitched *The L Word* anywhere other than Showtime. Showtime already stood alone as the network that offered the best and most varied movies featuring gay characters. I had worked with Showtime on other difficult and controversial projects, and I knew that my colleagues there would share my ambition to tell our lesbian stories frankly and honestly, without pandering and without hiding. When the then president of Showtime programming took me aside at the 2000 Golden Globes and whispered in my ear, "I think we're going to try that little lesbian show with you," I knew that I would need the kind of support I had gotten from Showtime on our movie that subsequently that night received a Golden Globe Award. I knew that I would need Showtime's brand of collaborative creative freedom in order to achieve anything like what I hoped to achieve.

What neither Showtime nor I knew was that the audience for our "little lesbian show" would comprise such a large, diverse, and passionately engaged assortment of people. Neither could we have foreseen that our show would become part of a larger cultural phenomenon. We never imagined that "the L word" would be used as a catchphrase in op-ed journalism, a rallying call for community organizing and an organizing principle in a host of serious sociological academic papers, the namesake for various women's health initiatives, and an epithet in a disastrous presidential election in which gay Americans were pilloried to divide and conquer an already dispirited electorate.

Equally, I couldn't have envisaged working with a cast of actors like the cast we've assembled for *The L Word*. They care deeply about these characters they've helped to bring into existence and about the stories we are telling. They participate earnestly (sometimes vehemently) with me and with the fantastically gifted writers and directors who come to work on our show. Together we find ourselves, often, in a collegial atmosphere of creative collaboration, workshop-

"We enjoy the passionate debate, the demands for representation, the appetite for greater diversity, the wishes for love to be requited and endings to be happy. Often they will. I promise."

ping, debating, analyzing, and processing character psychology and behavior (and perhaps also saving money on psychotherapy bills). Virtually every filmmaker who has come to direct an episode of *The L Word* has relished the creative freedom to bring her or his individual style and vision to our L world. All have remarked to me how smart and talented this cast is, and how like it is to making an independent film. Except for the fact that the crew is so capable, so prepared and confident and amiable, the machinery so well oiled, the ship so tightly run. I attribute that to the fact that *The L Word* is a women-driven operation. The way in which we collaborate is, I am told, highly unusual on a television series; it's also challenging and consuming and sometimes chaotic, and I attribute all of that to the fact that our whole project is created by and run by women. I believe that our fluid, ambitious, overachieving, chaotic woman-run mode and method accounts for much of what is successful about *The L Word*. And I believe, as well, that it accounts for the caliber of directors and guest stars, musicians, and personalities who have approached us to be on the show and/or readily accepted our invitations to come and join us in our endeavor. We all love what we're doing, and we know how privileged we are to be given the opportunity to go on doing it.

We're grateful most of all to the fans who support us; we know that they are ultimately responsible for conferring on us that ongoing privilege. We welcome the criticism along with the enthusiasm. We enjoy the passionate debate, the demands for representation, the appetite for greater diversity, the wishes for love to be requited and endings to be happy. Often they will. I promise. And even when they're not, I hope that we are all together in celebrating the fact that these stories are finally getting told and that lesbians are seeing their own lives reflected back at them in the entertainment culture that they have contributed to and helped to create.

Looking at the Big Picture (on the Small Screen)
How *The L Word* Is Changing the World

t has been over two years since television history was made with the premiere of Showtime's series *The L Word* on January 18, 2004. Nearly a million viewers tuned in to the pilot, making it one of Showtime's most successful programs ever. Many of us will never forget what we felt during the opening sequence, as Marianne Faithfull rasped about "so much love," the Los Angeles skyline whirred past, and two women spooned in bed, entangled in the sheets. Here at last were the stories of lesbian lives being played out in front of our eyes by an exceptionally beautiful and talented cast: Jennifer Beals and Laurel Holloman as a couple determined to have a family, even as they struggle to connect. Erin Daniels portraying a professional tennis player terrified of coming out on the courts. Mia Kirshner playing Jenny, a young writer whose life is forever changed by a kiss with an exquisite intellectual café owner (Karina Lombard), who makes her reconsider her commitment to her boyfriend (Eric Mabius) and the safety he provides.

The show debuted more than twenty years after the introduction of the first regularly featured lesbian character to daytime television—Donna Pescow's Dr. Lynn Carson in ABC's *All My Children* in 1983—and sixteen years after the first lesbian couple, Marilyn McGrath (Gail Strickland) and Patty (Gina Hecht) in a prime-time drama, ABC's *HeartBeat*. Since then, we've seen a smattering of lesbian and bisexual characters, but there wasn't a single main player among them until Ellen DeGeneres came out on her self-titled sitcom in 1994, transforming it into a show *about* a lesbian, albeit a rather sexually inactive one. With the identification of Sapphically inclined characters, we've also witnessed a continuum of girl-on-girl kissing over the years that began with a chaste dry-lipped peck on *L.A. Law* in 1991 between actresses Michele Green and Amanda Donohoe and has slowly progressed over time on *Roseanne, Friends,* and *ER,* to some more satisfying, realistic face-on-face action on *Xena: Warrior Princess, Buffy the Vampire Slayer,* and *Queer as Folk.* Still, American audiences had little sense of lesbian lives, because we weren't front and center.

Let's face it: We were desperate to see and be seen, and anyone who could sate our starving television appetites would be an instant heroine, a true trailblazer. But if that show didn't sustain us with compelling story lines and authentic, soulful characters, we'd lose interest and resume our usual activity of parsing other programs for lesbian subtext until something better came along. But Ilene Chaiken set the bar high with her show *The L Word* and consistently and courageously continues to raise it with each episode, creating a program that resonates with a broad audience; entertains, enlightens, and evolves over time; introduces a range of characters, some with whom we can easily identify, and other, more provocative characters who inspire us to reconsider our preconceived notions about gender, relationships, sex, and family.

Drawing in devoted viewers week after week from all over the world—twenty-five countries to date—*The L Word* is the word on *everybody's* lips, extending far beyond the lesbian community, defying demographics because the many different lives Chaiken has imagined are so fully realized on the small screen. Her unique observations, culled from twenty-five years of living in Los Angeles as an out lesbian, have largely informed her keen storytelling abilities, which she infuses with droll humor and genuine pathos. So, if viewers are not falling in love with one of the *L* women, many of us feel as if we are seeing versions of ourselves enacted on the set. And we can't stop talking about it to each other. It's become a full-on phenomenon: Just take a look at the traffic on Showtime's *L Word* message boards (per month, it averages more than 300,000 unique visitors to the site and 100,000 postings); the innumerable unauthorized *L Word* sites and blogs on the Internet; the high volume of features, essays, profiles, op-ed pieces, and reviews of the show in the mainstream, entertainment, and gay magazines and newspapers—*New York, Vanity Fair, Vogue, Entertainment Weekly, The New Yorker, People, TV Guide,* and *The New York Times*; and the increasing number of talks and papers that use the show as a springboard to discuss critical and cultural theory at academic conferences across the country.

Viewers love to unpack the psyches of the characters and disentangle their intertwined dramas, extol the show's virtues, and occasionally take it apart. The chatter is nonstop. "I knew when Maureen Dowd casually mentioned *The L Word* in her *New York Times* op-ed column about George Bush that we had arrived and that this thing was more than just a television show," said Matthew C. Blank, chairman and CEO of Showtime Networks Inc. These *L* women have crept into our imagination and taken hold—much in the way that Madonna did in the late twentieth century.

Chaiken first casually pitched the idea of a lesbian series to two Showtime executives she knew when she turned in the draft of her screenplay *Dirty Pictures* (2000), about the Cincinnati museum director who went on trial for exhibiting Robert Mapplethorpe's sadomasochistic photographs. At the time, they told her it was a great idea, but they thought the show would never fly. The entire landscape changed a short eighteen months later: *Will & Grace,* once the gayest thing on television, had the stakes considerably raised with the premiere of Showtime's sexy *Queer as Folk,* which went where no gay man (or lesbian, for that matter) had gone, at least not on American telly. At the

> **"Let's face it: We were desperate to see and be seen, and anyone who could sate our starving television appetites would be an instant heroine, a true trailblazer."**

Golden Globe ceremony that year, Chaiken got the green light from Jerry Offsay, then the president of Showtime Original Programming, for a more formal pitch she'd done. Several hours later, she snagged a Best Picture Golden Globe for *Dirty Pictures.*

With her characters and stories already mapped out, Chaiken needed to assemble her cast and crew. Actress Jennifer Beals was the first to sign on, followed by Rose Troche, who was hired to direct the pilot (she also serves as a writer and coexecutive producer). It was crucial that the show strike a balance between LA glamour and dyke authenticity ("They're not mutually exclusive," says Chaiken) and portray all aspects of lesbian sexuality with unflinching candor, because it is integral to who we are, and it is the aspect of our lives that has, by turns, suffered erasure and been the most mythologized. Blank says it is Showtime's mandate to "turn toward worlds, characters, and concepts that you just can't see anywhere else. The ideal show for us is the kind where, when someone gives you the one-line synopsis, you exclaim, 'Whoa! That's really interesting!' and then see it executed brilliantly. That certainly holds true on every level for *The L Word.*"

There is no singular lesbian narrative, and *The L Word* is a testament to the richness and diversity of the lesbian community. The ten female characters we've met in the past two seasons are very different from one another: Two are half sisters, one of whom is straight. The women are African-American, Latina, Jewish, WASP. One woman grew up in foster care and on the streets, while another was raised in a privileged two-parent home. They are hairdressers, art curators, aspiring writers, trust fund babies, café owners, musicians, professional athletes, journalists. They are also polyamorous, monogamous, hypocritical, righteous, modest, faithful, honest, treacherous, confused, butches, femmes, tops, bottoms, wealthy, and barely scraping by. Some have survived violations by men and by women. Two have struggled with drugs and alcohol. But they have in common love: a need for it and a capacity to give it.

Since the show's debut, *The L Word* has featured an A-list roster of guest stars cast in unforgettable roles—the late Ossie Davis as Melvin Porter, the father of Bette (Jennifer Beals) and Kit (Pam Grier); Kelly Lynch as trans-man Ivan Aycock; Rosanna Arquette as irresistible high-powered Hollywood socialite Cherie Jaffe; Anne Archer as Lenore Pieszecki, the mother of Al-

"As much as it's our show and we're telling our stories, it does in some sense belong to the lesbian community."

ice (Leisha Hailey); Snoop Dogg as hip-hop star Slim Daddy; Lolita Davidovich in the role of the possessive yet polygamous costume designer Francesca Wolff; and Camryn Manheim as hotheaded Hollywood producer Veronica Bloom. In its second season, *The L Word* turned up the volume politically—with cameos by pundit Arianna Huffington and feminist icon Gloria Steinem—and musically, with live performances by such acts as punk-disco burlesque artist Peaches and rock veterans Heart.

And while political story lines have a strong presence—among them, an anticensorship battle between the curator of an art show and a Christian Right group, the limitations of domestic partnership laws when a separated couple explores custodial rights—Chaiken's pen is not pushed by a heavy hand. Her obligation, she feels, is "to tell our stories with authenticity and above all, to entertain and keep it dynamic." Politics is a major part of our lives, too, and because of it, "we definitely get to bring up subjects that are important, and bring somebody like Gloria Steinem into this universe and introduce her to a world of young women who might not know that, if not for Gloria, we all wouldn't be here," says Chaiken. But the mere act of telling these stories is political, and just as the magazine was the medium in the late twentieth century for Steinem, the television drama has the capacity to be a powerful medium with which to dispel myths, disseminate information, and put forth the message in the twenty-first century.

With the show's critical and commercial success, Chaiken is fast becoming a feminist icon in her own right. Her renown isn't limited to the screen, either. She, together with the cast of *The L Word,* has participated in benefits for the Human Rights Campaign (HRC), the Gay and Lesbian Alliance Against Defamation (GLAAD) and Power Up, and served as the grand marshal of the 2005 San Francisco Gay Pride Parade. She also makes herself available to fans by maintaining an open dialogue with them through the message boards and taking their feedback into consideration. "As much as it's our show and we're telling our stories, it does in some sense belong to the lesbian community. Our fans are welcome to take the show and run with it in the way that they do. The viewers and I are in a very good conversation and, with this show in particular, it's a cultural conversation," she says.

Blank marvels at all that Chaiken is able to accomplish with *The L Word,* especially its ability to hit at so many levels. "At its most surface level, these are really attractive people leading some melodramatic lives, and it is interesting to watch for that reason alone. And yet on the other level, it is deep. It is provocative. It is literate. It is all of those things," says Blank. "Within the same week, we had the *New York Daily News* and *The New Yorker* writing about the show, and I love Ilene's ability to span that spectrum. I think that's part of the show's strength, and I know that's why there's such a broad, strong audience for it."

L Is for
Los Angelenas
(and a Few Los Angelenos)

Bette Porter
played by Jennifer Beals

Jennifer Beals was the first cast member to sign on to *The L Word.* A Chicago native, Beals began her acting career after high school graduation when she nabbed the lead role in *Flashdance,* which earned her a Golden Globe nomination and an NAACP Image Award for Best Actress. More recently, Beals has had starring roles in a number of films, including *Twilight of the Golds,* for which she won the 1998 Golden Satellite Award, *The Anniversary Party, The Last Days of Disco, Roger Dodger, In the Soup, Four Rooms, Vampire's Kiss, Doctor M., Caro Diario, The Madonna and the Dragon, Catch That Kid, Runaway Jury,* and *Devil in a Blue Dress.*

O n the surface, Bette Porter's tenacity, ambition, and confidence appear like arrogance, which serves her well in the viciously competitive art world, where she once ran her own gallery and now fights to keep—and ultimately loses— her director position at the California Arts Center (CAC). And while she can be self-righteous, self-involved, controlling, and obstinate, beneath it all she is insecure, lonely, terrified of failure, and deeply loving, even if she has trouble conveying it to those closest to her heart. In this respect, she is a lot like her father, Melvin Porter, an African-American doctor who loves his daughters but whose devotion to traditional values has often impeded his ability to connect with them even as he lay dying from advanced prostate cancer. Melvin's elusive approval may be what Bette longs for most.

Bette is defined by her work and rarely loses sight of her goal—to catapult the inconsequential CAC into the league of the MoCAs and MoMAs of the world, even if it means defying the mandate issued by the CAC board of directors and going head-to-head with her boss, Franklin Phillips, which it often does. Being unyielding in her quest earns her the admiration and respect of people like benefactor Peggy Peabody, and the ire of Peggy's daughter, Helena. It does nothing to help her in her personal life, no matter how eager she is to rein in her volatile temper and become more flexible and attentive to the needs of others, especially her partner of eight years, Tina Kennard. She yearns to repair the frayed bond with her half sister—

Occupation
Director of the California Arts Center (CAC)

Bette's Chart Connections
Alice Pieszecki; Tina Kennard; Candace Jewell (Ion Overman); Starlight girl (Gina Holden, "Lynch Pin"); Megan Friedman ("Longing")

Bette Porter on Bette Porter

"[Benefactor Bernard Riddle] may be out of the CAC's league, Franklin, but he's certainly not out of mine."
—"Lies, Lies, Lies"

"I overestimated myself. Supporting us both financially, and then when we lost the baby, I thought that *I* had to take on the whole burden. I thought that *I* had to *absorb* your pain and ignore my own."
—"Life, Loss, Leaving"

"I've never been the uninvited guest. I always prefer not to go where I'm not wanted."
—"Labyrinth"

the legendary but troubled R&B singer Kit Porter—but can't resist criticizing her decisions in business and romance, not to mention her setbacks in her battle with alcohol. Bette, who is biracial, also feels a chasm widening between herself and Tina, who is devoted to the pursuit of motherhood but who initially expressed an ambivalence about using an African-American donor, which is just one of the concerns intensifying Bette's anxiety. Tina breaks off their relationship after discovering Bette's affair with Candace Jewell, and then hides the fact of her pregnancy from her for nearly five months. Their separation undoes Bette as she comes to realize how much she needs Tina and pursues her with unprecedented passion . . . and patience.

Kit Porter on Bette Porter

"I'm the one that always ran away, okay? But don't do what I did. Stay, hear me out, because I'm not going to say what you think I'm going to say. There's only one thing that cuts across all our realities. It's love. The bridge between all our differences. And you have so much love in your life. Why are you trying to tear down that bridge? Why?"
—"Pilot"

"My sister is a pootie-chasin' dog who deserves to be tied down and whupped upside the head, but it doesn't change the fact that she loves [Tina] more than she loves her own life. And [Tina] should finish punishing [Bette] and get back to figuring on how [they can] . . . live with one another for the next fifty years or more."
—"Life, Loss, Leaving"

"The world according to Bette doesn't have the same props it once did."
—"Life, Loss, Leaving"

Tina Kennard on Bette Porter

"I think you're right to have such strong convictions. It makes you who you are. It sets you apart. I love you for that."

—"Let's Do It"

"Bette's pretty wrapped up in herself. She doesn't always see what's right in front of her. It's a problem. It's *always* been one of our problems."

—"Labyrinth"

Jennifer Beals on Bette Porter
Q & A

You were the first to sign on to *The L Word*. What drew you to the role of Bette Porter?

The writing and the potential for the character. I read the pilot and I was told to look at either Bette or Tina, and I gravitated more toward Bette. I thought it would be fun to play the dysfunction, that tension between appearing to be so unapologetically confident, and in reality, being quite diffident and vulnerable.

What do you like best about Bette's character?

The balance of the self-righteousness and the vulnerability, that they both exist in such large quantities in one body. That balance serves her sometimes—like the time Faye Buckley's people are out on her front lawn. If she had been less self-righteous, less sure of herself, there's no way she'd be able to come out on the lawn and confront those people. She's very capable of standing up for herself, which I appreciate, and she's able on occasion to be open and recognize when things are expansive in her heart.

Some things you might not have known about Jennifer Beals . . .

Incredibly versatile in her talents and tastes, Jennifer is an accomplished black-and-white photographer who is rarely without one of her cameras. She is also a devoted fan of the television series *Buffy, the Vampire Slayer.*

Jennifer says:

"I knew *Buffy* had become an addiction when I'd be shooting a scene, and the clock would creep toward 11:00 p.m., and I'd get resentful that I was at work missing *Buffy* reruns."

Bette and Tina are the two most politically active characters on the show. What is it like to play someone who gets caught in the political crossfire of a censorship battle with the Christian Right, as Bette does in the first season?

It's interesting to me to be able to play a character who can embody the implicit politicalization and also literally enter into that realm, to be able to take the fight from the inner circle to the outer circle. But even more compelling to me is the fact that this show is political in and of itself, even if none of the characters were to have any kind of political agenda at all.

How do viewers respond to you when you see them at an event?

Often women will come up to me and say, Thank you for representing us. It's interesting because, sometimes I feel like, yes, they're saying thank you, but they're also saying, Thank you for carrying this load that no one else was willing to carry, as if somehow, at one time it would have been burdensome. But what they don't realize is that I've been given this incredible gift: As an actor, I get to play an increasingly complex role that I love, and as a person, the playing of this role and the import of the show itself gives me, and my cast mates, and the crew, quite frankly, a sense of agency.

Tina Kennard
played by Laurel Holloman

T ina has only ever fallen in love with one woman in her life, Bette Porter—she left her entertainment-lawyer boyfriend for her—and has been totally devoted to her for the past eight years. But since putting her successful career as a film development executive on hold to prepare for pregnancy, Tina has been worried about the direction their relationship has taken. She would have never predicted that electing to carry their baby would result in a steady, semiconscious slippage into traditional heterosexual roles, with Tina as the passive wife and Bette as the domineering husband. With this power shift grows a widening gulf between them that they both try to deny. But when Bette sets Tina up with Marcus Allenwood—a sperm donor whom she's never met—and fails to mention that he's African-American, the problems between them become impossible to ignore. Bette interprets Tina's discomfort as a rejection of her biracial identity, while Tina is increasingly frustrated that her words are falling on deaf ears. She just longs to reconnect, and it is proving harder to do, even with the help of couples therapy.

Tina miscarries the pregnancy, and the ensuing anguish provides the two women a chance to get closer. Instead Bette shuts down, wholly immersing herself in the preparations for the "Provocations" show at the CAC, where she begins an affair with the contractor installing the sets. Left to grapple with her loss alone, Tina busies herself with volunteer work at the Headquarters for Social Justice. Finding out about Bette's indiscretion feels like the worst kind of betrayal. Devastated and

Born in Chapel Hill, North Carolina, Laurel Holloman was trained at the Piven Theater Workshop and got her start as a New York stage actress. She has appeared in more than twenty feature films, including *Boogie Nights, Prefontaine, Committed, The Incredibly True Adventures of Two Girls in Love, The Myth of Fingerprints, Lush, Cherry,* and *Loving Jezebel.* Holloman also had a recurring role as a tough and sexy vampire slayer on the series *Angel.*

13

Occupation
A onetime development executive in the film industry, Tina now volunteers as a grant writer for the Headquarters for Social Justice

Tina's Chart Connections
Bette Porter; Helena Peabody

Tina's Off-the-Chart Connection
Eric (Kyle Cassie, "Looking Back")

enraged, Tina moves out, with a secret of her own: She's pregnant again. As Bette pleads for forgiveness, and the stunningly beautiful but overbearing newcomer Helena Peabody makes a play for her heart, Tina decides what she needs most is to regain her autonomy.

Tina Kennard on Tina Kennard

"I'm going to do everything right. I'm going to be as together about this [pregnancy] as Bette is to her work."
—"Lies, Lies, Lies"

"I'm on the twelve-step program for people who are addicted to domesticity."
—"L'Ennui"

"I think, God, am I going to go to my grave and Bette will be the only woman I've ever slept with? But then, I look at her, and think, What more could I want?"
—"Looking Back"

"Look, I've been taking care of people my whole life. It's about time I started to take care of myself . . . Bette and I need to be on equal footing before there is any chance that we could work anything out. I need my autonomy."
—"Lap Dance"

"I'm gonna have a baby. I thought it was gonna be mine and Bette's, but it's going to be my baby. And I am going to love her, and care for her, and I am going to give her a great shot at life."
—"Loneliest Number"

Bette Porter on Tina Kennard

"You know, ironically, I was actually pleased to see that she had put on weight 'cause I thought, number one, it means that if she's eating to cover her pain, then she's really actually still in love with me. And two, if she's overweight, then maybe she might have trouble finding someone else."

—"Lap Dance"

"She doesn't belong to me anymore. Like it feels someone else had been touching her and making love to her, and I *felt* that other person and I felt her connection to that other person, you know? And, and she did things that we had never done together. And it was like she was so free . . . I always treated her so gingerly, you know, like she was some fragile thing. And now, even though she's pregnant, it's like she's unbreakable."

—"Late, Later, Latent"

Helena Peabody on Tina Kennard

"You're one of the few people who hold your own with [my mother]. Everyone else just fawns all over her. It's tedious."

—"Lacuna"

Jenny Schecter
played by Mia Kirshner

Mia Kirshner began her acting career at seventeen, playing a clairvoyant dominatrix in *Love and Human Remains*. Kirshner will be in Brian De Palma's forthcoming *The Black Dahlia* and has appeared in *Century Hotel, Exotica, The Grass Harp, Mad City, The Crow: City of Angels, Saturn, Spencer, Dark Summer, Anna Karenina,* and *Murder in the First.* She has also appeared on the television series *24,* where she portrayed a mysterious would-be presidential assassin.

Jenny has traveled across the country to West Hollywood to be with the person who makes her feel safest in the world: her boyfriend, Tim. She arrives with little more than a laptop filled with stories of her fictional alter ego "Sarah Schuster" in various states of completion and, unbeknownst to Tim, a treasure trove of unspeakable secrets she is far from ready to reveal. Within moments of first looking into Jenny's big blue eyes at Bette and Tina's party, Marina senses that Jenny yearns for a side order of danger, too. And while it's true that Jenny once boldly probed some of the darker realms of her psyche under the guidance of her writing mentor, Nick Barashkov, those explorations and adventures were primarily confined to the realm of her imagination and the pages of fiction she presented to him. But when Marina and Jenny share a kiss in Bette's and Tina's bathroom, the young writer sees her life going into a tailspin, forcing her to reckon with herself. Her passion for Marina is undeniable, but pursuing an affair with her means risking the loss of the one stable relationship she's ever had. And when things explode with Marina *and* with Tim, Jenny is left alone to contend with the heartache and an overwhelming identity crisis in a place that is not yet home. She feels totally unmoored.

That burden is eased by a developing friendship with Shane, who has become one of Jenny's two new roommates. Their bond lends her the confidence she needs to make friends, face the critical feedback of caustic writing instructor Charlotte Birch, and ultimately embark on a cathartic, soul-

Occupation

An aspiring writer, she supports herself with odd jobs, among them grocery clerk, diner waitress, ghostwriter, and stripper

Jenny's Chart Connections

Marina Ferrer; Dana Fairbanks; Robin (Anne Ramsay); Carmen de la Pica Morales

Jenny's Off-the-Chart Connections

Tim Haspel; Nick Barashkov (Julian Sands); Gene Feinberg (Tygh Runyan, "Locked Up," "Limb from Limb," "Life, Loss, Leaving")

Jenny Schecter on Jenny Schecter

"Autobiography of Red, Eros the Bittersweet. I think, um, those books practically changed my life."
—"Pilot"

"I can't be around you, anymore. It's confusing to me and it makes me feel insane."
—"Longing"

"I'm terrified of being on my own. I just gotta make myself do it, Robin, and I can't distract myself by creating all this fucking labyrinth-like drama that I'm so good at creating, and I promise you that you do not want to get sucked into my fucking bullshit."
—"Lap Dance"

"I think that if I were a guy, I would *definitely* ask myself out as a woman, and if I were a woman, there's no fucking way that I would ever ask myself out as a woman."
—"Loneliest Number"

searching journey that includes an exploration of her sexual identity and an excavation of her Orthodox Jewish family's history. She tentatively pursues Carmen de la Pica Morales, who, Jenny comes to realize, uses their relationship to keep tabs on Shane. Jenny becomes increasingly ambivalent about having her as a girlfriend as she watches Shane and Carmen try to resist each other, and she encourages the two women to get together. Jenny won't let anything compromise her friendship with Shane, especially as she confronts the pain of her sexually violent past, memories of which are dredged up when the third roommate—a videographer named Mark—violates them by placing hidden cameras throughout their house. But not even the most vigilant friend can't prevent Jenny from taking a self-destructive detour that begins with her stripping at a seedy go-go bar and ends with a frightening self-cutting incident.

Mia Kirshner on Jenny Schecter
Q & A

How much of yourself do you bring to Jenny?

Ilene [Chaiken] and I have always had a really good dialogue about where Jenny's going. We were pretty clear about the story of Jenny's rape and the impact that it has on you when you find out about that as an adult. We talked about that a lot. There are definitely similarities between Jenny and me with respect to us both being Jewish, as well. My grandparents are Holocaust survivors, so that was pretty important to me.

Jenny is one of the most provocative characters on the show. Viewers have responded to her with a mixture of empathy, frustration, and anger. What do you make of the audience's response to your fictional alter ego?

So many people seemed to have personal attachments and such strong feelings about Jenny. During the first season, some women wrote things that were absolutely correct, because even

I thought Jenny's behavior was deplorable. She was not being truthful, and she was being too much of a victim. But at the same time, I supported those moral ambiguities in the character, very much so. And then there were times I thought some of the postings were just downright mean. But the highlight of the whole show is reading those boards and especially during the second season, when women would write about their experiences of being violated in some way. It felt like these women were writing from a place of truth and power and I felt very gratified about being able to tell a story in a way that was brutally honest. The story we told through Jenny wasn't glossy, and that was great.

Do you like Jenny?

Now I do, very much. And I really respect her a lot. I always understood Jenny more than the audience did [*laughs*], but when we meet Jenny for the first time she seems very naïve, self-involved, confused, and a bit treacherous—*not* manipulative. I think she's one of those people that follows her instinct at the spur of the moment and doesn't really think about the consequences of her actions, but now I'd want Jenny as a friend. She's weird, and I think that she stands up for what she believes in. She's not a coward. I think that she has grown up so much since the series began. I think that she's worked very, very hard on herself and is still struggling with her own issues.

The shooting schedule in Vancouver can have you here between four and six months. Since none of the cast is from here, I would think that you all bonded pretty quickly.

We know each other's moods so well. I especially know Kate, Leisha, Erin, Pam now very much so, and Jennifer. You can just tell what they're thinking without them having to explain or say anything. These girls rock. In the first year, Leisha and I lived together; and then Kate, Leisha, and I lived together the second year. It takes me a long time to become friends with people. During the pilot, Erin, Leisha, Kate, Karina, and Laurel hung out together every night, and Jennifer joined them a lot. I didn't really. I was on my own for the majority of the pilot because I'm not great with big groups.

Where do you like to go in Vancouver?

On my own, I like to have dim sum in Chinatown. Kate, Leisha, Erin, and I like to go to this Belgian place called Chambar. It's pretty chic. The walls are painted red and there's exposed brick and the food is delicious. All of us eat at Natural Garden, a macrobiotic restaurant, which is pretty fantastic. After work we sometimes hang out at Leisha's house, just reading and talking

Tim Haspel on Jenny Schecter

"You scare me sometimes. I see you going right to that edge, and I think I've lost you. And then you come back with [this manuscript] and I know why you have to disappear on me like that. I'm so fucking proud to have you in my life."
—"Pilot"

Gene Feinberg on Jenny Schecter

"That's it! I'm sorry to break it to you, but you are a girl-loving, full-on lesbian!"
—"Life, Loss, Leaving"

Charlotte Birch on Jenny Schecter

"You are a compulsive excavator of your own emotional navel lint. A nit-picking, obsessive truth teller."
—"Late, Later, Latent"

Carmen de la Pica Morales on Jenny Schecter

"Jenny wouldn't know what the real deal was if it bit her in the ass. She is so . . . lost in her own darkness. I think she likes it in there."
—"Late, Later, Latent"

and having coffee or wine. My friend Libby, who is a trained chef, was living in Vancouver, so I also had tons of dinner parties at my house. It was actually one of the best things about our time there—having everybody come over and have this delicious food that a friend cooked and sharing great food with friends.

What do you do in your trailer during downtime between shoots?

I read. And at night we dance a lot. We turn out the lights in our trailer. I put on The Cure, Madonna, David Bowie, The Bronski Beat. We make up dance routines. A lot of times these impromptu dance parties were in my trailer because I had these tacky eighties mixes. I remember the first year, Leisha, Kate, and I went to Erin's house and we made up the craziest dance routines. It was so innocent and sweet and *so* the antithesis of cool.

Were you actually choreographing your moves? Borrowing material out of old videos?

Yeah, that and *Solid Gold.* Everything. I think sometimes when people meet Leisha or Kate, they look so cool and maybe unapproachable. But the truth is, we're all massive silly nerds. [*laughs*] It was a festival of geekdom.

Some things you might not have known about Mia Kirshner . . .

Mia studied Russian literature at McGill University. She is an avid reader: her favorite writers include Philip Roth, Mary Gaitskill, Leo Tolstoy, the graphic novelist Phoebe Gloeckner, and the lyrics of songwriters Leonard Cohen and Nick Drake. A cinephile, she also loves the work of actresses Isabelle Huppert, Charlotte Rampling, and Isabelle Adjani.

Shane McCutcheon
played by Katherine Moennig

Katherine Moennig originally hails from Philadelphia and has worked in theater and on film. She will appear in the upcoming films *Dead Girl's Diary* and *Art School Confidential* and has also been featured in *The Shipping News, Love the Hard Way,* and *Invitation to a Suicide,* and in the series *Young Americans* and *Law & Order: Special Victims Unit.* In addition, she was the lead actress in the music video "Is Anybody Home" for the band Our Lady Peace. On stage, she has acted in *As You Like It, Comedy of Art, The Theory of Total Blame,* and *Morning in the City* at the Williamstown Theater Festival.

S hane has made it her life's goal to travel light. A talented hairstylist on the rise, she opts out of schmoozing the Hollywood A-list and even quits a lucrative job as an assistant to the high-powered studio executive Veronica Bloom, who has the temperament of a land mine. She prefers to hang out at The Planet with her friends Alice, Dana, Jenny, Bette, and Tina and prowl for girls at the local club, Milk. One of the few people in the world who can keep a secret, and endowed with a rare gift for observation, Shane often intuits things about her friends that they don't yet realize about themselves. As devoted as she is to her friendships, however, Shane recoils at the mere prospect of a relationship—she can't even bear sleepovers during a one-night stand—because the threat of love is so daunting. Just because she swaggers with cool detachment and is able to fit all of her belongings into her rundown Toyota pickup doesn't mean she lacks baggage. In fact, its weight occasionally overwhelms her, even as her friends and a few of the many whose hearts she's broken offer to help relieve her.

But Shane is determined to go things alone. She prides herself on the self-reliance that enabled her to prevail through the anguish of being abandoned by her drug-addicted mother, and moved from one foster home to the next until she

Occupation
An up-and-coming Hollywood hairdresser

A Sampling of Shane's Chart Connections
Lisa (Luciana Carro, "Pilot"); Lacey (Tammy Lynn Michaels); Kelly (Stefanie von Pfetten, "Lagrimas de Oro"); Cherie Jaffe (Rosanna Arquette); Carmen de la Pica Morales

ran away at the age of ten. Her judgment isn't always sound: she's lived out of her car, passed herself off as a twink male hustler tricking along Santa Monica Boulevard, done copious amounts of cocaine and OxyContin—all risks she's willing to take. And when married Hollywood socialite Cherie Jaffe swoops into her life and knocks her off her boots, she thinks she might be ready to give love a whirl. But just as Shane finally opens her heart, Cherie's college-age daughter, Clea, unwittingly sabotages the affair with an explosive and untrue disclosure that turns the Jaffes against her. Reeling from heartache, Shane shuts down emotionally and swears off love forever. And then she has sex with Carmen de la Pica Morales, a persistent romantic who insists that she reconsider. But she's not yet ready to let down her guard and instead nudges Carmen in the direction of her new roommate and best friend, Jenny. Not until she watches the videos Jenny seized from her other roommate, Mark Wayland—a voyeuristic videographer, who had been spying on the women with hidden cameras—does she recognize how hardened she has become and resolves to give love another try.

Katherine Moennig on Shane McCutcheon
Q & A

Shane is the resident butch on *The L Word.* You've played androgynous characters before—Jake Pratt on *Young Americans* and the male-to-female pre-op transsexual Cheryl Avery on an episode of *Law & Order: Special Victims Unit.* Were you apprehensive about playing another gender-blurry role?

No, not really. If it's a good role I'm going to take it and let the chips fall where they may. It is true: All the roles that I have been noticed for happen to blur gender, but those are the ones that grabbed me and that I found the most interesting out of all the things that I've done. They actually had something to say. I don't have any interest in the surface pretty-girl roles, the one who lives next door to the protagonist. I think they've been done so many times, and I personally don't want to see another one, nor do I want to play one. So when characters like Shane

Shane McCutcheon on Shane McCutcheon

"My entire life, people have said that I would become a psychopath if I didn't learn how to feel . . . But I wanna know . . . what the fuck is so great about feeling? Because I finally let myself. And I feel like my heart's been completely ripped out."

—"Limb from Limb"

"Love's a bitch. I'd rather just have a good time and move on."

—"Life, Loss, Leaving"

"I would fuck myself, but I wouldn't date myself."

—"Loneliest Number"

"I don't need a dick to fuck a lot of girls."

—"Lynch Pin"

"The most important thing is to listen [to girls]. You get them talking, and you start hearing about their life, and then you figure out what they want. But you do not talk too much. That's the thing. Talking too much can kill it. You don't tell your life story, and you don't let them tell theirs."

—"Lagrimas de Oro"

"The thing I like about confession is, you don't have to see the other person's face. And you don't have to see how hurt they are when they realize that you can't be that thing they want you to be."

—"Loyal"

Bette Porter on Shane McCutcheon

"Have you ever noticed that every time Shane walks into a room, someone leaves crying?"
—"Pilot"

Dana Fairbanks on Shane McCutcheon

"Every single thing about the way·you're dressed, like, screams 'dyke.' "
—"Pilot"

Alice Pieszecki on Shane McCutcheon

"Oh my God! It's Yoda."
—"Pilot"

"She's like the only person on earth who can actually keep a secret."
—"Luminous"

Tina Kennard on Shane McCutcheon

"She has the best nipples in town and she knows it."
—"Pilot"

Jenny Schecter on Shane McCutcheon

"You just sometimes remind me of guys I used to date in high school."
—"Loneliest Number"

come up, I want to grab the opportunity. I'm not going to carry on playing these roles, and I might have put myself in a box a bit playing these characters, but I don't care because it's gotten me where I am now.

There are many notches in Shane's headboard, but only two women have won her heart. What do you think of Carmen and Cherie?

I love Carmen, and think she is a great person for Shane. She is the light where Shane is the dark, but I gotta say, I think Cherie Jaffe stole her heart.

Shane has a virtuous soul, as she demonstrated when she forgives the unforgivable: Mark's violation of her privacy in the one place she's felt at home. How can she remain friends with him?

I think deep down, she's violated just as many people as he has. To her mind, she feels like, I'm going to accuse you of doing this when I look at the things that I've done to people? Since when am I the upright citizen here? She doesn't get on her soapbox because she doesn't have one to stand on. She feels strangely empathetic, and I think she understands the emotions behind what he's done.

Veronica Bloom on Shane McCutcheon

"You know how to talk to people. It's a very rare and special skill."
—"Lynch Pin"

Carmen de la Pica Morales on Shane McCutcheon

"I know how hard you work to keep yourself at a distance from everyone else on the planet, but it's not working for you anymore."
—"Late, Later, Latent"

You make your home in Los Angeles, but filming the show can keep you in Vancouver for nearly half of the year. What do you like about living up north?

Everything is so close. I barely drove when I was in Vancouver. Leisha and I lived a few blocks from each other in this great neighborhood called Yaletown, which is all lofts, posh little boutiques, and great restaurants. Rodney's is this rustic oyster house that has the best food in the city. They always play Van Morrison, James Taylor, the *Boogie Nights* soundtrack, and other great music that makes the atmosphere; and all the guys that work there are just so handsome and sweet. We have gotten to know all of them, because we eat there at least once a week—they're the only friends we have in Canada that aren't involved in the show. Our big thing out here are dinners. We are always having dinner together. It's hard to do during the week because of our schedules, but we go out to eat with whoever is around that night, and if we are all in town during the weekend we go to someone's house—it usually ends with some kind of dance-off. We have such a blast together. I don't think I laugh more than when I'm with Erin, Leisha, and Mia.

What do you do in your trailer in your downtime?

I try to nap, but just when I'm in the perfect sleep mode, I'll get a knock on the door calling me to the set. So my fail-safe option is bringing a movie with me to work, like *Jaws* or *Singles*. During the first year, Erin, Leisha, and I watched *Goonies* and other eighties films. This year, I brought my Xbox to work, and Leisha and I played. I also got the *Lost* boxed set and tried to watch as many episodes as I could before they called me to set.

Some things you might not have known about Katherine Moening. . .

Katherine is an avid surfer. "I love it," says Katherine. "I try to surf as much as possible when I'm in LA." And, according to Mia Kirshner, Katherine likes to perform off the set for her friends. Mia boasts that her cast mate knows all the dance moves from Janet Jackson's video for "If."

"One night at my place," recalls Mia, "everyone came over and we were listening to Janet Jackson. When the song came on, Kate did the whole dance routine. She's going to kill me for revealing this [*laughs*]."

Ilene says:

When Ilene Chaiken first laid eyes on Katherine, she knew she had found Shane.

"Shane was very vivid for me. I knew who she was, how she felt, and I knew she would be very hard to find because there aren't a lot of girls out there who had that very particular vibe and look and presence. When I saw Kate Moennig's casting tape for the first time, I went, 'Oh my fucking God, there she is! Shane!' It was like she was Shane manifest, which was not the case for most of these other characters."

Alice Pieszecki
played by Leisha Hailey

Leisha Hailey graduated from New York's American Academy of Dramatic Arts. She has appeared in television commercials and was featured in the independent film *All Over Me*. Until recently, her focus has been on music: she was one half of the now-defunct pop-rock duo the Murmurs, with whom she recorded three albums for MCA/Universal Records during the 1990s. She made her television debut with *The L Word*.

Everyone at The Planet lives for the wit and wisdom of Alice Pieszecki, *the* go-to girl for information, not to mention the most dependable source of advice and support. A vigilant researcher, an expert eavesdropper, and a great confidante (with the caveat that she can't keep good news to herself for very long), she knows what Peggy Peabody spent on her whirlwind art-shopping spree, where to get the cheapest Botox injections, and how Tina figured out that Bette was cheating on her. She even has a hunch about the scheming Tonya and her role in the death of Dana's beloved cat, Mr. Piddles (even if it is fueled by a tinge of jealousy). Alice is also the person who introduces newcomer Jenny to Marina (for better or worse), helps Dana come out to her parents, and provides Tina with a couch and a shoulder to cry on when she and Bette break up. So, who better than Alice to compose all the "best-of" lists for *LA* magazine and chronicle everyone's sexual liaisons on an ever-growing chart (with Shane as a major hub) to make a larger statement about the human spirit?

If only Alice could apply her gift for shrewd observation and news gathering to her own life. The resident bisexual among her lesbian crew, Alice brags about looking for the same qualities in a man as in a woman, but how discriminating is she when her infatuations include the mean-spirited cad Gabby Deveaux and a hypersensitive, New Agey lesbian-identified man who calls himself "Lisa"? Things are made all the more difficult by her actress mother, Lenore, an insecure woman with narcissistic delusions, who frequently calls on Al-

Occupation

Journalist for *LA* magazine and host of *The Chart* radio program on KCRW

Alice's Chart Connections

Bette Porter; Gabby Deveaux (Guinevere Turner); Dana Fairbanks; Tayo (Martha Jaciubek, "Looking Back")

Alice's Off-the-Chart Connections

Lisa (Devon Gummersall); Andrew (Darrin Klimek, "Luck, Next Time")

Alice Pieszecki on Alice Pieszecki

"I am looking for the same qualities in a man as I am in a woman."

—"Pilot"

"We're all connected . . . Through love, through loneliness, through one tiny, lamentable lapse in judgment."

—"Let's Do It"

"Most girls are straight until they're not. And then sometimes they're gay 'til they're not."

—"Let's Do It"

"I've had enough drama and mindfucks, and women are fucking crazy . . . I could use a little nice, uncomplicated, boring, boy-girl sex masquerading as love. It's fine with me."

—"Lies, Lies, Lies"

"I don't want a lesbian boyfriend . . . I want a boyfriend who's straight, or I want a lesbian who's a girl!"

—"Luck, Next Time"

Lenore Pieszecki on Alice Pieszecki

"You could take a little more time with your face, you know. You might have a girlfriend by now."

—"Lies, Lies, Lies"

ice to bail her out of the huge bills she's run up at five-star hotels. No sooner does she save her mother than Lenore is scrutinizing Alice's appearance and trying to woo her friends. But jealousy, not Lenore, is what may be to blame in dooming Alice's romantic life, especially when it comes to her best friend, Dana, whose engagement to Tonya calls Alice's feelings into question. The two women, who once vowed never to sleep together, soon find themselves entangled in a hot, clandestine affair that morphs into a relationship when Tonya leaves Dana for Melissa Rivers. But because they never discuss the risk it poses to their friendship, neither is prepared to handle Kit's hiring of Lara Perkins as the new chef of The Planet, which awakens Dana's unresolved desires, elicits Alice's envy, and has the potential to devastate everything they hold dear.

Leisha Hailey on Alice Pieszecki
Q & A

Alice is such a good friend to everyone. Do you like her as a person?

Yeah, I love her. In a way, I wish that I had the quick wit she has. She always has the perfect thing to say even when she thinks she doesn't.

Alice is always up on everyone's sexual history, creating The Chart to illustrate the interconnectedness of the activities of her and her friends. Why do you think it's so important to her?

I think it's interesting that Alice chronicles everyone's sleeping patterns [*laughs*] because it's a really cool thing in life. We should all sit down and do that, because a lot of people have six degrees of separation between them. In the gay community, it's so small to begin with that it's pretty easy to stay on top of it. It's pretty shocking to think how insular it is. It's hard to walk into a room and not to have hooked up with one person, usually.

Alice has not had an easy time of it in the romance department: Gabby Deveaux ran roughshod all over her, and on the other side of the spectrum is clingy Lisa, the lesbian-

Gabby Deveaux on Alice Pieszecki

"Do you have to do everything your friends want you to do? Oh yeah, you do."

—"Let's Do It"

Bette Porter on Alice Pieszecki

"You and I dated for six weeks. It was never gonna go anywhere. I did us both a favor."

—"Lap Dance"

Dana Fairbanks on Alice Pieszecki

"Just 'cuz you're riding the big fat weenie doesn't mean there's something wrong with the way the rest of us do it, okay?"

—"Liberally"

"Alice, you're a funny lady, and it's one of the things I love about you, and I'm not the only one."

—"Loyal"

Tonya on Alice Pieszecki

"That's why you're so mean! You miss [Dana]! I barged in and I stole your best buddy. Look! Dana loves you! But I want you to know, Ton-Ton knows how to share."

—"Loneliest Number"

"I don't understand you bisexuals! I mean, *really,* make up your minds already."

—"Labyrinth"

Some things you might not have known about Leisha Hailey . . .

Leisha is an out lesbian—the only one on the principal cast. She originally auditioned for the role of Shane McCutcheon.

identified man. Who of Alice's lovers was the biggest head trip?

Lisa, for sure. I really had to wrap my head around that one because I've never met a lesbian-identified male, and I really felt that it was a sweet thing about Alice that she had the ability to take this odd person and find the best of them, and understand them and completely fall for what they were throwing at [her]. I like that she was so open to it, when everyone else was like, What? That's a nice quality.

Do you think Alice gets a raw deal?

Yeah, I think she's there for her friends a lot more than they are there for her. And that's really sad. She's a great friend. That probably goes back to The Chart thing, where she has this giant understanding of how in the end we're all still going to be connected in some way. She's really good at figuring things out for everyone else. But when it comes to herself, she's terrible at it.

Dana Fairbanks
played by Erin Daniels

Erin Daniels played Michael Vartan's mistress in *One Hour Photo* and starred in Rob Zombie's *House of 1000 Corpses*. She also had a recurring role on the critically acclaimed NBC series *Boomtown* and Fox's groundbreaking comedy *Action*. A St. Louis, Missouri, native, she now lives in Los Angeles with her two dogs.

She might be sure-footed on the court, but up-and-coming tennis star Dana Fairbanks worries that she is fumbling in every other realm of her life. She is eager for a girlfriend, but terrified of coming out, using her acid wit—and occasionally even trotting out a beard, her doubles partner Harrison Landy—to steel herself against the rejection she anticipates from the straight world, her fans, and especially her Republican parents. Her best friends, Alice, Shane, Bette, and Tina, try to ease the anxieties perpetuated by her agent, Conrad Voynow, who has her convinced that being out will destroy her career. Not even the adorable "soup chef" Lara Perkins—the sous chef at her tennis club who has won her heart with specially grilled vegetables and intense multiple orgasms—can coax the insecure athlete out of the closet. Subaru gives her the opportunity she seeks when they offer her a contract to be the spokesmodel for their Get Out and Stay Out ad campaign, catapulting her into the national spotlight by turning Dana into the "lesbian Anna Kournikova." She feels triumphant as she fires Conrad. But her younger brother Howie is taunting her. Dana's parents are mortified. And worse yet, Lara is long gone.

When Dana picks up a Human Rights Campaign Award at the Kraft-Nabisco Professional Women's Golf Tournament in Palm Springs, she is greeted by Tonya, a bulldozing guest liaison determined to hitch her wagon to a Sapphic celebrity. Flattered by the attention and awed by Tonya's buoyant authority, Dana quickly proposes marriage, much to everyone's

Occupation
Professional tennis player

Dana's Chart Connections
Lara Perkins (Lauren Lee Smith); Jenny
Schecter; Tonya (Meredith McGeachie);
Alice Pieszecki; Ralph (Tara Wilson,
"Looking Back")

Dana Fairbanks on Dana Fairbanks

"Look, if I'm outed, I'm screwed, Alice, all right? Sponsors aren't exactly clamoring to have their stuff repped by big ol' lezzie tennis players."

—"Pilot"

"Every time I'm attracted to somebody, she's either unavailable or straight."

—"Pilot"

"I've only slept with two girls my whole life. And I swear to God, if you repeat that I will have to kill you."

—"Pilot"

"Why can't I just be a second-rate tennis player who's famous for being a lesbian? That's okay with me, really, it's fine."

—"Lacuna"

horror. For Alice, that revulsion is unexpectedly compounded by heartbreak: She realizes she is in love with her best friend. As Dana prepares for her wedding to Tonya, eventually winning her parents' blessing along the way, she begins an illicit affair with Alice. Their trysts help her to discover the distinction between love (something she has for her best friend) and gratitude, which she feels toward Tonya, who has helped her find the courage to be true to herself. Dana later learns she's even paved the way for Howie, who surprises her with the disclosure of his own homosexuality. When Tonya leaves her for Melissa Rivers, Dana has the chance to be with Alice out in the open. But falling in love is not the hard part. It's relationships that require so much work, especially when Lara Perkins's new job as the chef at The Planet arouses Dana's old desires.

Erin Daniels on Dana Fairbanks
Q & A

Dana has evolved a lot since we met her two seasons ago, from a closet-case tennis player reluctantly deferring to Alice for wisdom, to becoming a nationally recognized lesbian role model who is on the verge of breaking Alice's heart. Despite her newfound confidence, she never totally sheds her insecurities, which is why viewers have such an easy time identifying with her. What is the secret to making Dana so lovable?

I really wanted to make Dana as human as possible, because she is funny and goofy, sarcastic, kind of rude sometimes, but she only does it because she's insecure. She's a dork, and I loved embracing that, because we all are. She is also sensitive and vulnerable. But Dana's goal is to be as normal as she can be, and to figure out what "normal" means. It's all about fear. Fear is what makes us who we are. Her fear was that she'd never be loved or understood, or that she could never be herself. But she found love. She came out. She moved on. She lost love and she found it again. The second season for Dana was more about becoming empowered and being comfortable with who she is. And I think a lot of it had to do with being with Tonya, who was a yes-man in a sense, but she was also somebody that took care of her. Dana felt safe with her, and it opened up a whole world for her, and she grew some self-confidence. She had a sort of a teacher-student kind of a thing with Alice because Alice always knew way more than Dana did about pretty much everything. Or at least it felt that way, until Dana had the courage to say, "Yeah, I know."

We meet three of Dana's girlfriends, two of whom are easy to love, and one who is incredibly entertaining to watch. Did you have a favorite?

I can't pick favorites! [*laughs*] Seriously, all three of the women I worked with are very different women, and they're very different actors. Meredith McGeachie, who plays Tonya, is great. Our scenes together were so funny, and I just knew that whenever we'd get to work, we'd have a good time. Lauren really brought out a softness because she's delicate and strong at the same time, so all of the stuff that I had with her was so dramatic. Leisha and I work really well together—we play off of each other. Sometimes you find another actor and there's a chemical re-

Alice Pieszecki on Dana Fairbanks

"Y'know, you are gonna pickle in that self-loathing homophobia, I swear."

—"Pilot"

"You look *hot* . . . I mean, from the neck up. I mean, we really gotta do something about your clothes. Gotta take her to Fred Segal."

—"Liberally"

"I guess like most things that are in front of your eyes, you don't see just how wonderful they are until they're gone."

—"Lap Dance"

Lara Perkins on Dana Fairbanks

"You are really, really gay . . . When you hide that, you're hiding the best part."

—"Lawfully"

Sharon Fairbanks on Dana Fairbanks

"We all have feelings for our girlfriends, Dana. It doesn't mean you have to act on them."

—"Listen Up"

action: You can just sit down with them and the scene just sort of runs itself. It's really sort of organic. The first kiss that we had to shoot was totally weird, in fact, because we'd become such good friends [*laughs*], and I was like, Ahhh! I'm making out with my best friend! And then we got over it. Clearly we got over it, because we were doing it all the time during the second season.

The L Word is the first lesbian serial drama, and participating in a groundbreaking project like this is exciting, but it also comes with daunting responsibilities because lesbian viewers have waited forever to see their lives represented in this format. When you signed on to the show, did you realize that you were accepting the chance to make history?

I did, and I was excited by it. I knew it was this chance to do something that was sociopolitical and that was anthropologically important, and you don't get that in television very often at all, if ever in your career. That excited me about it, to do something that actually changed the fabric of television.

How has being Dana impacted your life?

My taste in clothes is more expensive [*laughs*]. Seriously, it's made me more aware of women's issues, of lesbian and gay issues. At the same time, I don't know how it's impacted me because I don't know who I would've been if I hadn't played Dana. It's kind of hard to answer. I'm sure it's impacted me in many, many ways. I just don't know just how much yet because it's just been a huge part of my life for three years.

Some things you might not have known about Erin Daniels . . .

Erin's favorite aspects of the show are "any fun scenes with Kate and Leisha. That was Dana and *The L Word* for me: the three of us having a good time." Erin did her senior thesis at Vassar on Mies van der Rohe and collects midcentury modern furniture. Erin says, "I'm crazy-obsessed with furniture. My whole kitchen is like a paean to midcentury modernism."

Kit Porter
played by Pam Grier

Pam Grier achieved fame soon after she began her acting career in the early 1970s when she starred in such films as *Coffy, Foxy Brown,* and *Sheba, Baby.* In the 1990s, she made an impact as the title character in Quentin Tarantino's *Jackie Brown* and was nominated for Golden Globe, Screen Actors Guild, and NAACP Awards. She also received nominations for an Emmy Award, Image Award, and Black Reel Award. Grier's feature film credits include *Holy Smoke, In Too Deep,* and *Snow Day.* She recently starred in the television film *First to Die,* and had a recurring role in *Law & Order: Special Victims Unit,* among other programs.

Life hasn't been easy for legendary R&B singer Kit Porter—not since childhood, when her father, Melvin, an African-American doctor, left her mother for a white woman. Through most of her adult life, Kit has been trying to numb that pain and rage with drugs and alcohol, which have taken a devastating toll on her career and her relationships with her son David and her half-sister Bette. Now in her late forties, Kit is ready to reckon with herself and repair some of the damage.

Bette hasn't been making Kit's job very easy. She not only harbors years of resentment and hurt for the innumerable times Kit failed her, but she has become as recalcitrant as their father, who won't even tell her when he's in town. Her son David refuses all communication with her. Her luck begins to turn when hip-hop star Slim Daddy (Snoop Dogg) samples her 1986 hit, "It's the Real Thing," and has her star in the video. Then she is courted by Ivan Aycock, a recovering alcoholic trans-man she meets at a Drag King show at The Planet, who helps her find the courage to literally stick with the program— AA, that is—and turn her life around so she can begin to heal the fractures in her family relationships. Ivan becomes her silent partner at The Planet, and after a few self-actualization courses with the married Dr. Benjamin Bradshaw—delivered in lecture halls and over private, romantic dinners—Kit turns a modest café into a booming, innovative business. When her father is diagnosed with terminal prostate cancer, Kit joins

Occupation
Legendary R&B singer, occasional DJ, and the new proprietor of The Planet

Kit's Off-the-Chart Connections
Roger (Anthony Sherwood); Ivan Aycock (Kelly Lynch); Dr. Benjamin Bradshaw (Charles S. Dutton)

Kit Porter on Kit Porter

"Damn, what is it with you people and your need to take apart everything and process each little detail? If the dude wanna give up his white-man rights to be a second-class citizen, then hey, welcome to our world."
—"Losing It"

"No, the point is that you and David have been brainwashed by Melvin into thinking that I'm some kind of a falling-down drunk. I got it under control."
—"L'Ennui"

"I am [straight], but I don't need you to tell me that, and neither does Ivan. The way I see it, Ivan is the one who gets to say whether or not he's a man or a woman. And he's been telling me he's more of a man."
—"Life, Loss, Leaving"

"This is a dream come true. I've always wanted to have a place where musicians could come and jam and get much love."
—"Loneliest Number"

"I haven't slept with a woman and I am definitely a feminist."
—"Lacuna"

forces with Bette—who has been humbled by her devastating breakup with Tina—to care for him in his final days. Bette has developed a newfound respect for Kit, and she's not the only one: as Melvin lies on his deathbed, he marvels at Kit's success for the first time, giving her the encouragement and attention she's been craving her whole life.

Pam Grier on Kit Porter

Q & A

Kit has come a long way in two seasons, from struggling with alcoholism and getting stuck in bad business deals, to staying sober through AA and turning The Planet into a swank and profitable restaurant and nightclub. What do you think of Kit?

I love her. She's a mess, and I like playing her, and I love that she's courageous enough to admit her wrongs and live with the pain. She used to drink it away and now she's trying to tough it out. That's courageous, because you want to numb pain with drugs and alcohol, and she has found the maturity.

She's tried to stop drinking before. How was she finally able to stay sober?

She went to AA, and also meeting Ivan. She believed in Ivan, and believed that Ivan treated her better than any other man.

Kit later finds out that Ivan has had a long-term relationship with another woman while he was courting her.

He's a player. Here is this woman who is a man, who treated Kit like every other man in her life. How many times have we gone through that? Betrayal is going to happen. I really like that story line. The fact that Ivan helped her with her AA, and with the loan for The Planet. Bette couldn't help her with the loan—she's got a great job, but doesn't have that kind of money. Ivan helped her a lot.

Kit is a legendary R&B and soul singer who has transformed The Planet into a music venue where we occasionally get to see her sing with BETTY. You are also a musician. What has it been like to wear both hats?

It's fun. With music, you don't age. My taste in music ranges from classical to gangsta rap.

Does Kit's musical career take its cues from from any artists in particular? I thought I recognized a bit of Chaka Khan because of her versatility.

Kit is a composite of Minnie Riperton, Donna Summer, Patrice Rushen, Valerie Simpson, and a little Chaka Khan. Chaka because they parallel in a lot of her personal problems of drinking and addiction. Kit can do international music, and keyboards and R&B and Motown. She has an open ear for all music. She's ageless. Kit plays what the girls want in the clubs, but then sometimes during lunchtime there'll be Ravel. But at night, it's mosh time. She's really eclectic, like BETTY—their group is extremely eclectic. Kit reflects everyone's taste. She doesn't only have one style. If she had one style of music, she'd have one style of thinking and she would be very rigid and her character wouldn't be evolving and she wouldn't have a pulse on all the other characters.

What's the hardest thing about playing Kit?

Well, I don't drink, I don't do drugs, so to play someone who is that inebriated and lost would be very difficult, and I have to work on that. It takes some extreme technical work to make it seem real. Where does it come from? Why is she reacting this way? What's with the outcome? When she broke up with Benjamin, why didn't she break down and fall again? She set herself up with a married man, and she knew he wasn't going to leave his wife for her. Kit got tired of being on the side. Ivan misled her. But Benjamin didn't. He was upfront with her. It's been exciting for me to see Kit mature. You have to dig deep. You have to give things up. You can't be yourself. You have to be the actor and walk on thin ice and fall through and be able to get out.

Some things you might not have known about Pam Grier . . .

Pam is a huge horse lover and lives on a ranch with her three beloved dogs. She is a fan of country music and is a musician in her own right—she used to sing backup for Bobby Womack when she was a student at UCLA. Pam says, "Alan Jackson, Brooks and Dunn— some of the best country R&B you've ever heard. Alan Jackson is so fine. I'll listen to anything that says something about the human soul."

Bette Porter on Kit Porter

"You know, when I was a kid and I saw you onstage, I thought, That's my sister. She can do anything. I feel like that right now."
— "Loneliest Number"

"I do not think you are a fuck-up . . . I think you're amazing. You know, I see how you've turned your life around and I'm really in awe of how together you are these days. I just know the situation [with Benjamin]. And no matter what, there's always someone who gets hurt. And I just don't want it to be you."
— "Late, Later, Latent"

Melvin Porter on Kit Porter

"If you had lived some kind of life of decency and respectability, then possibly I would be your audience. But not now."
— "Lawfully"

Slim Daddy on Kit Porter

"Excuse me, kid. If it wasn't for Kit Porter, wouldn't be none of us here. Wouldn't be no song. Wouldn't be no video for you to shoot. So what you meant to say was, you fixin' to sit yo' ass over there and figure out how to get this right. Right?"
— "Luck, Next Time"

Ivan Aycock on Kit Porter

"[Marina's mom] may be a contessa, but as far as I'm concerned, Kit, you're a queen. Don't you forget it."
— "Life, Loss, Leaving"

Marina Ferrer
played by Karina Lombard

Karina Lombard moved to Barcelona as a young child, then lived throughout Europe and came to New York where she began modeling, dancing, and acting. She has appeared onstage in *Uncle Vanya, Cat on a Hot Tin Roof, Summer and Smoke, M. Butterfly, Joan of Arc, Betrayal* and *Danny and the Deep Blue Sea.* Lombard was also in the films *The Firm, Legends of the Fall, Last Man Standing,* and *Wide Sargasso Sea.* Most recently, she had a recurring role in the television series *The 4400.*

Marina is exquisitely beautiful, multilingual, erudite, sexy, and mysterious—in other words, the perfect seductress. And what could better appeal to a lonely, wide-eyed, Midwestern writer than to receive the unwavering attention of a charming, self-assured sophisticate? Marina had Jenny at the first utterance of "Nietzsche," sensing that the "straight" girl at Bette and Tina's party wasn't necessarily straitlaced. She may have taken a leap of faith by following Jenny into the bathroom and passionately kissing her, but her instincts weren't altogether off: Jenny kisses her back before fearfully pushing her away. The clandestine affair that ensues is perpetually on the verge of exploding, and while both enjoy a bit of risk taking, only Jenny believes she has everything to lose. When Tim discovers their secret, we learn that Marina cleaves to a couple of life rafts of her own. Hers appear in the form of her polyamorous partner, Francesca Wolff, a brash costume designer whose hard work finances all Marina's ventures, like The Planet and—unbeknownst to everyone except Bette and Kit—an estranged husband in Milan named Manfredi Ferrer, to whom Marina has been married for twelve years. When Tim confronts Marina, she refuses to take sole responsibility for the affair, sending him into a violent rage. To Tim, she appears remorseless and unaffected by the consequences of her actions. On the contrary: Soon after Jenny walks out on her, Marina loses Francesca, her business, her sanity, and nearly her life.

Occupation
Proprietor of the West Hollywood café
The Planet

Marina's Chart
Connections
Jenny Schecter; Francesca Wolff (Lolita
Davidovich)

Marina's Off-the-Chart
Connection
Manfredi Ferrer (Derek de Lint, "Lap
Dance")

Marina Ferrer on Marina Ferrer

"The Greek word *eros* denotes want, lack. The desire for that which is missing. The lover wants what it does not have. It is by definition impossible for him to have what he wants, if, as soon as it is had, it is no longer wanted."
                    —"Locked Up"

Jenny Schecter on Marina Ferrer

"Every time I look at you, I feel so completely dismantled."
                    —"Longing"

"She was possibly the most beautiful woman I'd ever seen . . . [and] she wrecked my fucking life with supposition."
                    —"Looking Back"

Bette Porter on Marina Ferrer

"I know it's not my place to judge you, Marina . . . and I don't know what's going on with you and Jenny, but I think this is wrong."
—"Let's Do It"

Tim Haspel on Marina Ferrer

"The woman has a charm that goes way beyond the fact that she's just . . . stunning."
—"Let's Do It"

"You preyed on [Jenny]. Pretended to be her friend! Playing your phony intellectual games just to get into her pants . . . You are fucking pathetic, Marina."
—"Losing It"

Francesca Wolff on Marina Ferrer

"She's beautiful, and that compensates for a multitude of sins."
—"Luck, Next Time"

"The thing about Marina is that when she focuses on you, you feel like you're the only one that exists. It's her gift."
—"Luck, Next Time"

Tim Haspel
played by Eric Mabius

Eric Mabius was born and raised on the East Coast and graduated from Sarah Lawrence College. He has starred in more than a dozen films, including *Resident Evil, Welcome to the Dollhouse, The Crow III: Salvation, Cruel Intentions,* and *Lawn Dogs.* He currently appears as Dean Jack Hess on *The O.C.* and has also had leading roles in *Eyes, Extreme Team,* and *Dancing at the Harvest Moon,* and guest roles on *Party of Five* and *Chicago Hope.*

Kindhearted and unassumingly gorgeous, Tim is a former Olympic swimmer turned California University coach who has eagerly awaited his reunion with his college girlfriend Jenny Schecter for six months. Jenny's skittishness can put Tim on edge, but he is ultimately trusting, which proves to be his Achilles' heel. An avid reader of her work, Tim understands Jenny's need for breathing room and has transformed the unused toolshed in the back of their modest West Hollywood home into a writing studio. Tim's affability wins him immediate friendships with his neighbors Bette Porter and Tina Kennard, and with their pal Marina Ferrer, the proprietor of The Planet café. But when Tim walks in on Jenny and Marina *in flagrante delicto* in the very studio he built for her, the betrayal feels as brutal as murder. And in a way, it is: he mourns the loss of a life he thought he would have and becomes enraged when he discovers that everyone at The Planet knew of the affair, convinced that he is the butt of a huge joke. Deceived by the woman he loves but feels he no longer knows, and, he believes, by a group of women who he thought were his friends, he leaves West Hollywood and takes a coaching job at Oberlin in Ohio.

Occupation
Swim coach at California University

Tim's Off-the-Chart Connections
Jenny Schecter; Trish Peverell (Nicole McKay, "Pilot," "Lies, Lies, Lies," "Lawfully," "Liberally," "Limb from Limb")

Tim Haspel on Tim Haspel

"I was the only idiot who had no fucking clue!"
—"L'Ennui"

Jenny Schecter on Tim Haspel

"I can't imagine my life without him. I don't want to imagine my life without him."
—"Longing"

"You're such a good man."
—"Locked Up"

Marina Ferrer on Tim Haspel

"I see what Jenny sees in you."
—"Let's Do It"

Carmen de la Pica Morales

played by Sarah Shahi

Sarah Shahi hails from Dallas, Texas, and moved to Los Angeles in 2000 after a chance meeting with Robert Altman, who was at the Cowboy Ranch shooting his film *Dr. T. and the Women.* The legendary filmmaker encouraged her to move to LA to pursue acting. A former member of the Dallas Cowboys Cheerleaders, she graced the cover of the infamous Dallas Cowboys Cheerleader Calendar in 2000 and embarked on a USO tour to entertain the troops in Bosnia, Macedonia, Kosovo, and Italy. Shahi will be seen in the feature film *The Adventures of Beatle Boyin.* She appeared in the feature film *Old School* as well as in such television series as *Dawson's Creek, Frasier,* and *Alias.*

Romance is DJ Carmen de la Pica Morales's favorite language, and candor is her idiom of choice. So how is it that she has managed to fall in love with Shane McCutcheon, a sexy player, whose idea of commitment is letting Carmen stay the night? Carmen, who lives at home with her mother, doesn't do casual sex on principle, especially not with damaged goods. But after hooking up with Shane a couple of times, she senses that there is more going on beneath Shane's cool exterior. Getting past Shane's steely reserve requires earning her trust—she has been hurt too many times to entrust her heart to anyone.

So it puzzles Carmen that Shane would get her a gig spinning records for Kit Porter at The Planet and encourage her to date Jenny, her roommate. These acts of altruism practically ensure their constant contact: If Carmen isn't working The Planet crowd into a froth with her intense drum-and-bass grooves, she is curled up with Jenny on their living room couch watching classic movies and trying not to watch Shane make out with other girls. Hanging out with Jenny is an ideal way to bide her time, not only because she grants access to Shane, but she provides pleasantly odd company. As Carmen and Shane play emotional chicken—exchanging surreptitious flirtations in the kitchen, baiting each other's jealous tenden-

Occupation
Production assistant by day, DJ by night

Carmen's Chart Connections
Shane McCutcheon; Jenny Schecter

Carmen de la Pica Morales on Carmen de la Pica Morales

"I'm not someone who falls for fucked-up, unavailable people."
—"Luminous"

"I was sixteen back then, and I fell madly in love with Lucia Torres. She was Pablo Fuentes's girlfriend. You just didn't fuck with Pablo's girl. But I did."
—"Late, Later, Latent"

"Do you know what's fucked up? You and I know what the real deal is. We saw it the first time we laid eyes on each other."
—"Late, Later, Latent"

Shane McCutcheon on Carmen de la Pica Morales

"It's hard for me to have you and Jenny in my face all the time."
—"Late, Later, Latent"

cies with public displays of affection for other girls—their feelings for one another become impossible to deny. Carmen is ready to declare herself, and dares Shane to open her heart and let her in.

Sarah Shahi on Carmen de la Pica Morales

Q & A

There was one interview with you last year in which you described an initial apprehension about being on *The L Word.* What inspired you to audition for the role of Carmen?

My words were misrepresented. It's definitely—knock on wood—the best job I've ever gotten and the easiest job I've ever gotten. When I auditioned, I went in on a Friday, and then by the following Monday morning, they asked, Can you be in Canada by Wednesday? I was never apprehensive of it or fearful of it. There was never a question of wanting to do it. It was the biggest opportunity I'd gotten thus far in my life. The shock was the move to Canada, which could have been in Lithuania, as far as I was concerned. I totally had to uproot my life for about six months to move to Vancouver. I'm just a little girl from Texas, so that was a life-changing thing.

Everyone from the cast hails from the United States or other parts of Canada, so being disoriented together for nearly half a year must feel pretty intense. But I would think that an ensemble show like this would inspire some serious bonding, or at the very least, camaraderie, or it wouldn't work.

Yeah, it's totally intense. And when you have an ensemble piece like this, if there's any animosity or tension between two or three cast members, it won't work. I think we are all quite lucky that there's not, because had it been any other set of eight or nine actresses, it could've happened. We all know that women can be catty, so I think we all got very lucky that it's not like that. I've gotta say, being on the show has been nothing but learning experiences—it's like I get to take an acting class every day. I love it.

Kit Porter on Carmen de la Pica Morales

"Carmen is *all* that."

—"Lynch Pin"

Jenny Schecter on Carmen de la Pica Morales

"It's okay that we're not meant to be together. And I know that the only reason why you're with me is because you wanna be near Shane."

—"Land Ahoy"

Carmen is at once incredibly sensitive and tough as nails. What do you make of her?

Carmen has much more of a temper than Sarah does [*laughs*]. She's pretty spicy. But I relate to her a lot. We're both very similar when it comes to feelings of the heart and work and her interactions with people: There is a niceness, and there is also this no-bullshit attitude. You don't play games with her. It's like, Well, this is how it is: I like you. You don't like me? I guess it's okay. I can go on, but I just had to let you know. I am very much like that. I feel all of her heartaches. I feel all of her joy. I totally get everything.

What has Carmen taught you about life?

The only thing that I would say I've learned is that gay culture is just like straight culture, so what is the big fucking deal? You know what I mean? They have relationship problems, marital problems, getting pregnant problems, adultery problems, they've got great love lives. Yes, you can fuck with a dildo, or sometimes you don't want to fuck with a dildo, you know it's just like every other relationship. At the end of the day, what's the big fucking deal?

Some things you might not have known about Sarah Shahi . . .

Sarah's paternal great-great-grandfather Fath Ali Shah Qajar was the Shah of Iran in the nineteenth century. And, like her fictional alter ego, Sarah is a film buff. Carmen's idol is Brigitte Bardot; Sarah's film idol is Katharine Hepburn.

Sarah says:

"Katharine Hepburn was a force every time she stepped in front of the camera. She was masculine, she was feminine, she was strong, she was weak, she was vulnerable. She was everything all in one. It seemed like she had an impact on every person that she met."

Helena Peabody
played by Rachel Shelley

Rachel Shelley hails from England, where she has appeared on television, in film, and in the theater. For her performance in the Academy Award–nominated film *Lagaan,* she was nominated for a Zee Cine Award (Indian Oscar) for Best Supporting Actress, which brought her to the attention of American audiences. Her other credits include *Seeing Other People* and the British movies *Sparkling Cyanide* and *Cruise of the Gods.* When Shelley is not working, she makes her home in London.

H elena Peabody is endowed with exquisite beauty, intelligence, power, and bottomless financial resources, but none of these has enabled her to attain what she longs for most: love. Her mother, the exuberant but emotionally withholding Peggy Peabody, hasn't set an especially good example. Peggy is as cavalier about romance—marriage is an institution she has never taken too seriously—as she is about her maternal obligations, believing that her daughter's devotion can be bought. The younger Peabody seeks psychiatric help to work through these issues, but neither she nor her shrink, Dr. de Obaldia, can resist the erotic potency of the transference dynamics in the office. Helena seduces her doctor, corrupting the sanctity of her treatment. When Peggy retires, she appoints her daughter as the new director of the Peabody Foundation. This inadvertently grants Helena the power to avenge her mother's parental negligence by redirecting the organization's focus toward social justice programs and away from Peggy's true passion, art.

Helena bestows a $100,000 grant on the Headquarters for Social Justice, and personally congratulates the author of the proposal, Tina Kennard, whom she finds impossible to resist. Tina is reeling from her recent breakup with Bette, the very woman who has won the maternal affections of Peggy Peabody. Helena perceives Bette as one of the many obstacles blocking her from one of the sources of love she craves, and she uses her every resource to dismantle her. Helena also finds Tina's pregnancy alluring—she tells Tina she is "sexy"—be-

Occupation
Director of the Peabody Foundation,
board member of the CAC

**Helena's Chart
Connections**
Dr. Isabel de Obaldia (Mimi Kuzyk,
"Lynch Pin"); Winnie Mann (Melissa
   Leo); Tina Kennard; Leigh Ostin
   (Cobie Smulders, "Luminous,"
   "Loud and Proud," "L'Chaim,"
   "Lacuna")

Helena Peabody on Helena Peabody

"I know I shouldn't have kept [my kids] beyond my curfew. I just get so carried away, you know? I want to give them something wonderful to take back to New York, something they can think about when they get sad, knowing their mummies are splitting up."
    —"Luminous"

"I've never actually attended a Pride parade before. I mean, I've had parties around it, I've rented rooftops with amazing views of it, but I've never actually been in it."
    —"Loud and Proud"

cause she longs to be intimate with a nurturing soul. She once realized this desire with her previous partner, Winnie Mann, a playwright with whom she's currently locked in a custody fight over their two young children. Helena initially bewitches Tina, but her demanding and elitist nature makes her lover bristle. As Helena's battle with Winnie grows more acrimonious, Tina pulls away from her. Much to Helena's horror, Tina begins to rebuild her relationship with Bette, who longs to coparent the child they planned together, and whose father has recently been diagnosed with terminal cancer. The fury that drives Helena to act out—parading women in front of Tina in an attempt to make her jealous—only serves to alienate her further from the woman Helena wants.

Rachel Shelley on Helena Peabody
Q & A

In England, you have primarily been cast in sympathetic, even fragile, vulnerable roles. So Helena Peabody, a beautiful, rich, cunning woman, is a bit of a departure. Where do you find Helena's edge?

I think for me it's whatever works, and it's a whole mixture of stuff. Watching Peggy Peabody was very good, like

Bette Porter on Helena Peabody

"The woman is a fucking dragon, and she's making my life a living hell. . . . She is a monster. However you wanna categorize it, she likes to fuck with people for sport."
—"Lagrimas de Oro"

Tina Kennard on Helena Peabody

"I don't think you're interested in sex unless there's some sort of risk or someone's watching or something else is going on!"
—"Late, Later, Latent"

Winnie Mann on Helena Peabody

"That's how she deals. She colonizes. . . . She'd never even thought about kids, but it was a dream of mine, and she's in the business of making people's dreams come true until she co-opts them and makes them her own."
—"Loyal"

Peggy Peabody on Helena Peabody

"I hear things are getting ugly between [you and Winnie]. I won't have that, Helena. Everything you do reflects on me. Please try to remember that."
—"Lacuna"

when she walks into the hotel with her dogs and gives one to Bette when they first meet, and everything is about me—that kind of thing I got from her. But then there are small things you can pick up. I had an old agent in London who had a very particular way of talking to people. Clients wouldn't see it, but you'd sometimes see it in the office when she was on the phone doing the deals.

Your role was to be Bette's greatest obstacle. Were you given a mandate to be mean?

When I came in, I had a role to play: to upset the apple cart. I had to be the worst rival to Bette and facilitate the breakup between her and Tina. A lot of the stuff I was doing was about my effect on people. But I played Helena with sympathy. I have to understand why she is the way she is.

And she definitely has a gentler side. Helena notices Tina's pregnancy right away, and tells her that she finds her body sexy. What is more winning than having a stunning woman like Helena make you feel beautiful when you're feeling so huge? She may be manipulative and covetous when she feels threatened, but she is also incredibly seductive and charming.

Helena's not done anything wrong, really. What did she do? She came to LA, she met some new people. Yeah, she has money, and she uses it in such a specific way, but it's part of her life, part of her upbringing. And here's Tina, this beautiful pregnant woman who is kind of a bit angry, ultimately. She's hurt by Bette. She's not fighting Helena off. And when Helena arrives in LA, Bette and Tina are not together anymore.

Tina is also likely drawn to her because her temperament feels familiar. Like Bette, Helena has ambitions to change the world for the better, yet she is also self-centered and can't bear to relinquish control. But Bette isn't calculating.

And there are other differences. For whatever reason, Bette pretty much gets a lot of what she wants, and when it comes to relationships, Helena hasn't really. She has to almost buy what she wants. Of course, that doesn't work when it comes to relationships.

Do you like the way Helena is evolving as we look ahead to season three?

Yes, I'm really enjoying it. Because six months have transpired between seasons two and three, by the time we get there, Helena has been California-ized a bit. We see a different angle to her, because she couldn't stay the pariah—it wouldn't seem real. If that was the case, who would be hanging out with her, anyway? She has to adapt to be included. So, the story being told is a different story, one that's as much about what's happening to me as what I'm doing to other people. It's much more interesting for me to play these different layers now.

Some things you might not have known about Rachel Shelley . . .

After earning an English degree at Sheffield University, she toyed with the idea of a journalism career. She spent her first few summers after college performing at the Edinburgh Festival. Rachel has chronicled her experiences working abroad on the film *Lagaan* and on *The L Word* for *The Guardian* in London. An avid reader, Rachel counts Ian McEwan (author of *Enduring Love* and *Atonement*) among her favorite writers and has most recently enjoyed *The Kite Runner* by Khaled Hosseini and *Two Lives* by Vikram Seth. She is also a huge fan of Ricky Gervais's comedic television series *The Office* and *Extras*.

Mark Wayland
played by Eric Lively

Eric Lively has a diversified portfolio. A professional photographer, he shot an Abercrombie & Fitch campaign, and as an actor he has appeared in music videos, television sitcoms, and feature films. He graduated from LA County High School for the Arts and later attended New York City's Parsons School of Design, where he studied photography. His television credits include *Minute with Stan Hooper, Uprising, Armed and Innocent, So Weird,* and *A Mother's Fight for Justice.* Lively's feature film credits include *American Pie* and the independent Showtime film *Speak.*

Mark Wayland is a voyeuristic videographer with grand ambitions to become a documentary filmmaker like his idol, Albert Maysles. He moves in with Shane and Jenny and becomes intrigued by the volume of Shane's girl traffic. Inspired by his new living situation, Mark decides to embark on an anthropological project: *A Compendium of Lesbianism.* But in order to get immediate funding for it, he has to assure his boss and investor, Eric Sonnenberg, that there will be pussy a-plenty. He interviews Shane, Jenny, and their friends about all aspects of lesbian life. While Jenny and Shane are out, Mark and his best friend, Gomey, secretly install hidden cameras throughout the house to capture the girls in action. Though initially disappointed to discover that they talk a lot more than they screw around, Mark finds himself, and in turn, his camera, becoming increasingly fixated on Shane's emotional life, which costs him his friendship with Gomey, and ultimately his deal with Eric. Jenny discovers the videos and busts him. Just as he readies himself to move out, he accepts Jenny's dare to stay and face the consequences. His violation devastates his roommates, but has a different impact on each: Shane watches the videos to review the errors of her ways and ultimately finds it in her heart to forgive Mark. But the intrusion conjures up repressed memories of sexual violence for Jenny, and in her rage she wages a war of piercing silence against him, before she suffers a mental breakdown.

Occupation

Videographer for a direct-to-video company that produces such fare as *Bareknuckle Backyard Wrestling* and *World's Craziest Bachelor Parties*

Mark Wayland on Mark Wayland

"I would love to ask for your forgiveness. I probably wouldn't forgive myself, so I don't know if you can relate to this, but it's like this terrible thing that I was doing suddenly became the best, truest thing that I had ever done."

—"Loud and Proud"

"When I moved in here, I was the type of guy who was capable of doing shit like this, but I am not that guy anymore."

—"Loud and Proud"

Gomey on Mark Wayland

"You're gonna fuck up this gig we've been working our asses off on for some chick? News flash, man! This girl you're crushing on is never gonna be with you! You've got a real live dick! And that disqualifies you from getting up in there!"

—"Loyal"

Jenny Schecter on Mark Wayland

"Mark, you're weird. You're weird, you're weirder than me!"

—"Luminous"

"You have violated us. You are violating us. You have crossed every line of trust. And don't you dare tell me this is for the sake of art."

—"Land Ahoy"

"It's not my job to make you a better man, and I don't give a shit if I've made you a better man. It's not a fucking woman's job to be consumed and invaded and spat out so that some fucking man can evolve."

—"Loud and Proud"

Landing on Earth...lings:
The Pilot

The L Word had a long gestation period before it premiered on Sunday, January 18, 2004, with the help of Executive Producers Larry Kennar and Steve Golin and Showtime, who gave Creator and Executive Producer Ilene Chaiken the go-ahead. Chaiken, Coexecutive Producer Rose Troche, and Showtime Senior Vice President, Talent and Casting Director Beth Klein reminisce about the pre-Word years.

It All Started Back in 1999 . . .

Ilene Chaiken: I wrote an article for *Los Angeles* magazine about the gay and lesbian baby boom in LA, which was inspired by the fact that my children were then two years old. I looked around me and every lesbian I knew was starting a family, and so were a lot of gay men. I wanted to write about this whole big movement of gays starting families, but I didn't think it was necessarily a subject for a movie. *Los Angeles* magazine hired me to write an essay about it, and in the course of writing it, I realized I was writing about my life, and about our community, and it wasn't just about lesbians and gay men having babies. We had an anthropological story in our community within the larger community, and there were details in our lives that hadn't been told in the mainstream venue—our stories were multitudinous and ripe for the telling. I very casually and whimsically proposed it to two Showtime executives—Joan Boorstein and Cindy Bell. I'd been working with them on my screenplay for *Dirty Pictures*. Showtime had just ordered the movie and it was going into production. It just seemed that a television series as a form lent itself naturally to telling stories of multiple characters, to making the point that our lives weren't monolithic. I wrote about ten pages, but it wasn't a TV show pitch. It was stories that happened to people I know: Here is a lesbian couple starting a family and what they went through, and here's the Lothario and some of the hearts she's broken, et cetera. It was very casual. These women, both straight, listened to me and said, "I love this. This is really fun. Never in a million years will we sell it to those guys around the corner." And I let it go.

But about eighteen months later, the whole landscape of TV changed. *Queer as Folk* was on the air. That's what I remember most distinctly, because I found out shortly after that Showtime was developing the English series as an American show, and it was very, very successful for them. *Will & Grace* was the most popular show on the air. Clearly things were changing, and with *Dirty Pictures* nominated for a Golden Globe, I decided to reapproach them. I went to a senior executive called Mark Zakarin and pitched it much more formally: This is the show, these are the characters. All of the characters that are in the show were in my pitch, more or less. It was a

"Mark Zakarin stood up at the end of the meeting and did something that rarely happens in my business: he said, 'We're going to do this. We have to.'"

little bawdy and audacious, and he was just tickled by it. He stood up at the end of the meeting and did something that rarely happens in my business: He said, "We're going to do this. We have to." Two days later, at the Golden Globe ceremony, *Dirty Pictures* won the Golden Globe, and I got the green light to proceed. I wrote a script.

The Real "L" World

Ilene Chaiken: I started out with the social world that I had lived in, in LA, for twenty-five years. I wasn't interested in representing specific people. I just wanted to represent types and experiences, and I also wanted there to be some diversity within the group knowing that our lives connect in all kinds of ways, and that our sexual orientation isn't the only link, but that it sometimes brings us together with people we might not necessarily have bonded with. At the same time as I wanted there to be some diversity within the ensemble, I wanted it to be real. I just said I'm going to start with this core group and tell some truth about it and not create some complete fantasy of rainbow-style diversity that doesn't exist anywhere. I know if we do this successfully and the stories feel real and authentic and we get to go on telling them, that we'll eventually be able to broaden the scope of the show and the characters who are represented for quite a long time.

"We took a look at Laurel and Jennifer together, and in two seconds we knew it was just magic."

The Title Report: Once Were *Earthlings*

Ilene Chaiken: Kathy Greenberg and Michele Abbott, my original two colleagues who share the creative credit on the show, came up with the working title. It was a riff that they did. I don't think it was theirs exclusively, but something that they had heard. "Is she an earthling, or just a visitor to the planet?" We shot the pilot with that title, and people were writing to various Showtime reps, asking why is it called *Earthlings*? But from the very beginning, we were told we weren't going to use the title because it codes as sci-fi. When you're trying to program a TV show you don't want to have to overcome a misconception.

Finding a Title That Reads Less Sci-fi and More Lesbodrama

Ilene Chaiken: For months and months, [the title] went back and forth to Showtime. They pitched ideas to me, and my ideas were always too high-flown for them, so they hired a company to do a title study and submitted twelve pages of appalling titles. It was really horrifying and if we didn't think quickly, the show was going to wind up being called something very cheesy. We were really down to the wire, and I said to my writing staff, "We're going to

spend the first half of the session brainstorming titles." We came up with a couple that we liked, along the lines of "The Field Guide to Gay Girls." Then [staff writer and actress] Guinevere Turner started talking about a bit that k.d. lang did at her last concert in which she did some kind of a riff on, "I'm a leh—, I'm a leh—"and I said, "Oh she couldn't say the L word." And then I thought, Oh, *that's* a good title. Put that on the list. I pitched it to Showtime, and I pretty much decided the minute I came up with it that that was it. Showtime was initially resistant, but we couldn't come up with anything better, and I think it's a really good title.

"I pitched it to Showtime, and I pretty much decided the minute I came up with it that that was it."

Piloting the Pilot: Hiring a Director

Ilene Chaiken: I hired Rose Troche to direct the pilot. We weren't necessarily looking for a director who was also a lesbian, but she had just done *The Safety of Objects,* which I thought was really interesting and sophisticated. We met and talked, and I really liked her and thought that it would be a great thing to have a director who was also a lesbian and who brought her own experience of being a lesbian. It's not just that she's a good director and does really great work, but it is good to have as many points of view to underscore the thesis of the show, which is that there's not just one point of view, there's not just one lesbian.

Casting the Line: The Challenges of Casting the Show

Beth Klein, Showtime senior vice president, talent and casting director: This was a tricky show to cast because, as with *Queer as Folk,* we had sexuality and nudity issues, and potentially straight people playing lesbians and lesbians playing straight people, so we had a lot of sensitivity from managers and agents about not wanting their clients to be on the show. Once we got beyond that hurdle, we wanted to put together an ensemble of stunning, unique, eclectic, and wonderful actresses. We were very pleased to have Jennifer Beals sign on, and later, for Pam Grier to join the cast. We built around that.

We saw a lot of people for the role of Tina. They narrowed it down to two, and decided to test chemistry. Jennifer was working on a film at the time, and she very graciously offered to have the two finalists come and hang out with her on the set. She said she didn't want to do an audition, and instead suggested that she and the other actress sit and talk to see if they have chemistry. That's not a normal thing to do, but because Jennifer was working, we took these two women out to her trailer on the film set. They each talked to her for about an hour and we filmed it. We took a look at Laurel and Jennifer together, and in two seconds we knew it was just magic. There was just instant chemistry there, which is something we don't always do. We don't always test that chemistry, and sometimes we've learned that we made a mistake and sometimes it works out fine. It's an exciting part of the process.

The Secret to Achieving Chemistry

Beth Klein: I think one of the things that contributed to the chemistry is taking a group of people away from their homes and sending them to live up in Canada. You bond in a different way and more quickly because you're all in this together, away from home, with a group of people, and in it for the same reason and all ready for success. Because you don't have those distractions to come home to or to your friends and your normal support group to take you away from it, I think they all got closer and bonded so quickly that it really added to what you saw on the screen. We got really lucky. We knew they were all talented, but you never know how it's going to come together, and that's a huge kudos to Rose Troche and Ilene Chaiken and producer Rose Lam. Once you have assembled a cast, what do you do with them? They made it brilliant.

Striking the Balance Between Glam and Lesbian Authenticity

Ilene Chaiken: There were a couple of things that I was looking for in one or two of the characters, and then in some cases it was just, Here's a story we're going to tell—someone come along and show me who she is. There is always a bottom line, though, which is completely intuitive, and it's a lesbian thing, and I think only other lesbians will know what I'm talking about, which is not that she has to be dyke-y. I could care less about an actor's actual personal sexual orientation. But you have to look at her and say, "Okay, I believe it." Sometimes an actress

"Sometimes an actress comes in, and however good she might be, you say, 'No way. She is not a lesbian in anybody's world.' "

comes in, and however good she might be, you say, "No way. She is not a lesbian in anybody's world." And sometimes you're wrong about that, because I've met some lesbians I've said that about. For the most part, we're just looking for a kind of authenticity that's very, very hard to articulate, but we know what it is. And there were definitely disagreements with Showtime about who the right choices were, but not because they wanted some straight male fantasy and I wanted dyke authenticity. There were one or two instances where they didn't get it. In one case, I remember saying, "I'm telling you guys that this is the only actress that I can even see casting this part. Trust me, please!" And then they came back to me and said, "Wow!"

Filling All the Slots

Beth Klein: We originally auditioned Leisha for Shane. Leisha came in, and it was one of those moments where we'd never seen her before—and no casting director can tell you they know every actor in town—and she was much more of a music person at that point. She came in and lit up the room. And although she was not ultimately what Ilene really envisioned Shane to be, we all said there has to be a place for her. She's so special and so natural, and all of a sudden, we all said, "What about Alice?" Because when Kate walked into the room, it was so ob-

"I didn't want it to be buxom babes. I wanted it to have a real range because whether you're talking about lesbians or gays or just people in general, they don't all look alike."

vious to me that she was Shane. She has a very unique look about her. I just thought, She is going to be the coolest character on the show if we have her. We set such a tone and the style and a reality, too. I didn't want it to be buxom babes. I wanted it to have a real range because whether you're talking about lesbians or gays or just people in general, they don't all look alike. I think we did a really good job of achieving that. Kate was instant, and Leisha, it was just so much "I want this person in my show." There was just an energy and a look and a uniqueness and a realness. Jennifer and Pam were straight offers. We'd already done a series with Pam called *Linc's,* and knew her and loved her from that. Laurel's work I knew from all of the independent features she'd done and loved her and was thrilled she wanted to do a TV series. I knew Erin from having cast her in another pilot a few years earlier, so that was fun. I'd been a fan of Mia's for a really long time. Jenny was one of the hardest parts to cast because it was such a delicate balance of innocence, but she couldn't be too sweet Pollyanna next door. She had to have all the subtext underneath it. Mia's got this wonderful edge to her, and those big huge beautiful eyes, and it's such an interesting combination. The role of Marina was also tough. Karina's one of those people who walked into a room and you went, Whoa! Once we had Mia cast as Jenny, that's when we went about casting her love interests.

The Pilot Takes Off—After a Few False Starts

Rose Troche, coexecutive producer: The pilot, which is considered episodes one and two, took twenty days of shooting—the first time around. We hired all of our crew and shot it in Vancouver in the summer of 2002. When we finished it and sent it to the network, they said, "Hey, the Kit thing—don't like." Pam Grier's Kit role was written differently. Originally, she was a lesbian performance artist and videographer and had The Chart tattooed on her back. It was an interesting idea, and Pam was ready to play a lesbian, but she was an outsider to the group and it wasn't really working. So Ilene and I had to come up with a new concept for who Kit was. Ilene had the idea, and I worked on it with her. And then we gave The Chart to Alice.

I think it was such a good move to recast her as Bette's sister. It brought up all of these other issues about race, from a black mother and father, and then you have the biracial sister, who is better educated and was more privileged and who the father is really proud of, but she's gay. And then you have these strange black sheep, so to speak. It was really great like that. Their resentment plays off one another. It's about lightness of their skin.

Showtime also didn't like Tim being an anthropologist, which was what he was originally, and he was played by Scott Bairstow. So we had to reshoot every scene that Kit was in—the party scene and any time you saw anything like that, we had to reshoot it. And then we had Tim become a swim coach at CU. Then we resubmitted it. But Scott wasn't a very convincing swim coach because he was too small, so we had to recast him. We were halfway into shooting Episode 103 when we auditioned new Tims. We cast Eric Mabius and then went back and reshot all those scenes in the pilot. We finished shooting the pilot and got the go-ahead for fourteen episodes total.

Season One
Episode Guide

At first glance, the L World seems seductive, harmonious, urbane, near-perfect. The opening scenes of the pilot show us a female couple—Bette Porter and Tina Kennard—awakening in bed, tangled up in the sheets and in each other, excitedly preparing to make a baby. Next door, we watch young swimming coach Tim Haspel put the finishing touches on the shed he's transformed into a writing studio for his girlfriend, Jenny Schecter, who is moving across the country to live with him. We laugh as three friends—closeted professional tennis player Dana Fairbanks, bisexual journalist Alice Pieszecki, and Casanova hairstylist Shane McCutcheon—gently sling witty insults at one another at their favorite café, The Planet, while the sultry European proprietor, Marina Ferrer, fills their espresso cups.

In the fourteen episodes of season one, two long-term relationships are put to the test and both collapse under pressure. For Bette and Tina, the obstacles are manifold. Bette has a tenuous grasp on her job as the director of the California Arts Center (CAC), where she's constantly at war with the board of directors who hired her to shake things up—but not too much. When she lands "Provocations," a high-profile, controversial art show, the CAC becomes a violent battleground with the Christian Right over First Amendment rights and the meaning of art. Bette struggles to make peace with her older half sister, Kit, a kindhearted, reckless R&B singer who has been battling alcoholism for years. The love between the two is palpable, but so are the years of resentment and mistrust. At home, Bette and Tina, who left her film development job to concentrate on pregnancy, worry that their respective goals are forcing them to lose touch with each other. Or is it that after seven years, the couple is simply growing apart?

No sooner does Jenny arrive in LA to be with Tim than she finds herself engaged to marry him and embroiled in an incendiary affair with the seductive Marina. The café owner may be predatory, but she recognizes that a young writer boasting a literary alter ego inspired by Nietzsche couldn't possibly crave safety, as Jenny earnestly claims. In this love triangle, no one is who he or she initially seems to be, and everyone stands to get burned.

Alice and Dana are constantly needling each other: Dana is mock-revolted by the fact of Alice's bisexuality, and Alice baits Dana to come out of the closet. But underlying the amusing barbs is a mutual deep-seated affection, heartfelt concern, and unrealized romantic desire. Dana—always the last to know everything—is awestruck by Alice's wisdom about sex and relationships . . . *other* people's relationships. In fact, Alice, a magazine writer who composes "Best of" lists for a living, documents everyone's past and present liaisons on a wall-sized chart in her apartment to prove her theory that we are all ultimately connected by love and desire. But she, with her claims of looking for the same qualities in a man as in a woman, is far less savvy when it comes to her own romantic interests, which tend to be fraught with neuroses no matter the sex. We gain insight into Alice's insecurities when we meet her mother, Lenore, who undermines her confidence at every turn.

At the behest of her manager, who is courting corporate sponsors, and out of fear of her Republican parents, Dana has been trying in vain to keep her lesbianism a secret from the world—that is, except from her friends at The Planet. Dana's manager has her convinced that being an out lesbian will kill her chances of getting an endorsement deal with Subaru, and she is eager to become the next Anna Kournikova—but she is just as eager to find a girlfriend.

Each of the eight women in *The L Word* endures a trial by fire in season one.

Falling for Lara Perkins, a.k.a. the "soup chef" at her tennis club, forces Dana's hand. She can have her dream girlfriend, but not if their relationship remains clandestine. Dana chooses her career over love, only to find she could have had both when Subaru proposes an ad campaign to turn the burgeoning tennis star into a lesbian athletic icon.

Love will find Dana again, but first she will have to come out to her Republican parents before the Subaru ad does it for her.

Shane likes to keep lesbodrama to a minimum by simplifying her populous love life: She prefers one-night stands and tries to avoid sleepovers, even as she leaves hundreds of broken hearts in her wake. But Shane's cavalier exterior belies her sensitive, vulnerable spirit. And much as she wants to remain emotionally detached, even the occasional illicit assignation can lead to love, as Shane learns when she begins an affair with married socialite Cherie Jaffe.

Each of the eight women in *The L Word* endures a trial by fire in season one. They take leaps of faith at work—jumping the fast track to become a hairstylist to the Hollywood A list or wresting a landmark show from a major museum—as well as in their personal lives. Alice is there, charting the names and connections to reflect the bittersweet and often serendipitous nature of their L World. But she, along with Shane, Tina, Dana, Marina, Bette, Kit, and eventually Jenny, are also there to help bolster their friends' confidence, assess situations, celebrate good times, and offer solace and support through the most devastating moments.

"The Pilot": Episodes 101 and 102

Teleplay by Ilene Chaiken

Story by Ilene Chaiken and Kathy Greenberg & Michele Abbott

Directed by Rose Troche

Aspiring writer Jenny Schecter moves to West Hollywood to be with her swimming coach boyfriend Tim Haspel after a six-month separation. Is the suburban neighborhood as "traditional" as Jenny thinks it is? Wait until boyfriend takes her to a party next door, at the home of Bette Porter and Tina Kennard. That fête sends Tim and Jenny into a tailspin. After seven years together, Bette and Tina are experiencing the itch,

This Is the Episode in Which . . .

- Tina introduces the concepts "bush confidence" and "nipple confidence."

- Bette and Tina encounter a potential sperm donor, a Frenchman who refuses to play by their rules of insemination and instead offers his own: "Ze penis. Ze pussy. Ze baby."

- Shane shows off her inner Yoda when she philosophizes about "the New Male": "The new male is more spiritual than the old male. He sees his sperm as an extension of his inner being, whereas the old male shot into any female without thinking about what would happen. The new male totally cares about what becomes of his seed."

- Marina Ferrer proves that the poetry of Anne Carson resonates like Barry White with the literarily inclined Sapphic set.

- Tim gets a lot of guilt-induced action from Jenny.

- Dana tries to invent a new catcall—"Cris-pay"—to the disgust of Alice and Shane.

- Dana and Alice make a halfhearted promise to never sleep together.

- We see The Chart on Alice's wall for the first time.

Music featured in these episodes:

"The Pleasure Song," Marianne Faithfull

"Serve It," Fundamental

"At the Speed of Light," Transientworld

"Chocolate Cake," Paloma

"Tragic Flaw," Suzanne Little

"Sadness," Transientworld

"Prodfill," Dan Gagnon

"Moon Burn," Moka Only

"Better Day," Sweatshop Union

"Lady Love," Joystick

"Acrobik," Dan Gagnon

"If I Had a Reason," Paloma

"Borrito," Fundamental

"Havana Disco Nap," Paloma

"Il Bambino," Chris Tarry Group

"Dee and Bee," Dan Gagnon

"Superclever," Kinnie Starr

"Pavlo," Adieo

"Gold n Green," Joystick

"Sun Again," Kinnie Starr

"How Long," Mr. Airplane Man

"Uchi Mata," Transientworld

"Up in the Room," Mr. Airplane Man

"Cannonball," Damien Rice

so they opt for a two-pronged approach to scratch it: couples therapy and artificial insemination. In that order and on the same day. They check in with LA's preeminent couples therapist, Dan Foxworthy (Daryl Shuttleworth), which reveals frays in their relationship that neither is ready to acknowledge, let alone address head-on. With Tina ovulating at full tilt, they have little time to spare, so they go on a sperm-donor crawl, beginning with an artist who boasts vibrant paintings and lackluster semen. Bette and Tina's friends at their local hangout, The Planet, suggest throwing a last-minute fiesta, in which guests bring a virile man to go along with the requisite six-pack. The Planet posse includes sexy rock-chick hairstylist Shane McCutcheon, whose entry into Bette and Tina's party involves spurning last night's one-night stand, Lacey, for a new conquest; an up-and-coming professional tennis player, Dana Fairbanks, desperately trying to pass off her queeny doubles-partner Harrison Landy (Landy Cannon) as her long-term boyfriend, even as he baldly hits on Tim; and Alice Pieszecki, a bisexual magazine writer who composes "Best of" lists for *LA* magazine and maps the romantic entanglements of her friends on a wall-sized chart in her apartment.

As Alice and Jenny settle in to a conversation about the writing life, Marina Ferrer—the stunning Italian proprietor of The Planet—saunters in with a look and a line that brush the love chronicler off the couch and sweep Jenny off her feet. How could the wide-eyed lit lover who had envisioned marrying Tim suddenly find herself infatuated with this woman? For starters, when Marina says, "Thus Spoke Zarathustra," it sounds like "Meet me in the bathroom."

Marina notices that the aftereffects of the party kiss have set Jenny in The Planet's daily orbit, so she starts inviting her to the women's party at the café, to an exclusive reading group, to dinner, to bed. Jenny initially resists these invitations but eventually accepts all of them and subsequently feels herself being "dismantled." And while the party failed to hook the hostesses up with the perfect donor, Bette believes she has scored one on the way to couples therapy: up-and-coming sculptor Marcus Allenwood. Tina isn't keen on the idea of bearing the child of a man she's never met but becomes downright distraught when Marcus shows up for their date at the Cryobank: Bette neglected to mention that he's African-American. Bette interprets Tina's hesitations about parenting a multiracial child as a rejection of her identity. Ironically, it is Kit, Bette's alcoholic half sister, who has the clarity of mind to lend some perspective to their situation, and, as we'll come to see, it is one of the few times Bette will listen to what Big Sis has to say.

Ilene Chaiken on Putting the L Women on the Couch

"We're telling our LA stories, and I don't know anybody who hasn't been in therapy, who isn't in it currently, and who doesn't have several therapists or at least who hasn't been through several therapists. When we look at our friends and our circle of acquaintances, everybody is in therapy, everybody has been medicated, everybody is dealing with her psychological baggage."

Lacey, played by Tammy Lynn Michaels

We first meet Lacey at Bette and Tina's party, confronting Shane about being blown off. Apparently, she was not apprised of the "McCutcheon House Rules": no sleepovers, no commitments, and rare is the repeat performance. Between Lacey's obsessive jealousy and Shane's cavalier approach to sex, theirs is a toxic mix, so it is no surprise that Lacey stalks Shane. But the anti-Shane campaign to "Stop the Menace"—complete with flyers and a banner—freaks everyone out. Shane knows how to stop it: lend her an ear and a roll in the hay. It works every time.

Tammy Lynn Michaels has appeared in the short version of Angela Robinson's film *D.E.B.S.* and the television series *Committed* and *Popular.* She is married to musician Melissa Etheridge.

"Let's Do It": Episode 103
Written by Susan Miller
Directed by Rose Troche

Tina decides to embrace Marcus as their donor, so she and Bette celebrate by making a romantic venture of the insemination at home. Alice tries to sell The Chart as a story idea to her *LA* magazine editor, but he likes her plan B pitch much better: vaginal "rejuvenation" surgery. The receptionist for LA's best vaginal rejuvenator just happens to be Alice's treacherous ex-girlfriend Gabby Deveaux, who doesn't have to beg Alice for another chance. Starting to sizzle both on and off the tennis court, Dana is not only being eyed by a Subaru ad representative but quite possibly by Lara Perkins, the adorable sous chef at her tennis club, who has been sending her complimentary plates of specially grilled vegeta-

This Is the Episode in Which . . .

- Alice and Shane start picking up on the sex vibe between Marina and Jenny, unbeknownst to the clandestine lovers.

- Dana inadvertently coins the term "soup chef."

- Bette and Alice have this exchange on monogamy, which will prove ironic by the season's end:

  Bette: *Why is it so important for you to believe that everyone is sleeping with everyone else?*

  Alice: *Because they are.*

  Bette: *No, that's just your little fantasy. Here is a truly radical idea for you to contemplate: Monogamy isn't just hypothetical. Some people actually do practice it.*

Music featured in this episode:

"Gold n Green," Joystick

"Waiting," Patric Caird

"Allegro Vivace," Mozart

"Masibodji," Alpha Yaya Diallo

"Futcher," Butter Chicken

"Blunt," Wild Strawberries

"Syrupsniph," Flunk

"Meneate," Rumba Calzada

"Tenos," Dan Gagnon

Karaoke version of "Baby Got Back," Sir-Mix-A-Lot

"Mi Manerade Amarte," Los Pinguous

"Esta Noche," Puentes Brothers

"Chameleon," Transient World

"Looks Just Like the Sun," Broken Social Scene

"Vintage Chemicals," Transientworld

"Let's Do It (Let's Fall in Love)," Ella Fitzgerald

Gabby Deveaux, played by Guinevere Turner

Deveaux must be French for "devil spawn," because Gabby is one manipulative, coldhearted chick. An aspiring screenwriter, she tries to play the soul mate card to curry favor with Alice. Gabby is reputed to be sizzling between the sheets, but after so much practice, let's hope so. Her expertise at game playing is what initially draws Alice in. Shane, Dana, Tina, and Bette find Gabby despicable for her lyin', cheatin', undermining ways, and finally get Alice to open her eyes and snap out of her Deveaux daze.

An actor, writer, and director, Guinevere Turner has appeared in nearly twenty films, and has written for two seasons of *The L Word,* serving as the show's story editor. She first came on to the film scene in 1994 as the star of *Go Fish,* which she cowrote with *The L Word*'s coexecutive producer Rose Troche. Most recently, Turner has collaborated with filmmaker Mary Harron on *The Notorious Bettie Page.*

bles. When Dana wants to know if unsolicited platters constitute flirting, Alice, Bette, Tina, and Shane realize that their hapless jock friend lacks gaydar and come to her rescue. Dana is mortified when her friends embark on a mission at the club to suss out the sous-chef situation. But Lara's appearance and behavior at work leave few clues about her sexuality—not even Shane, who has the ability to melt the heart of the most unresponsive straight woman, can get a pulse on her. Just as Dana is feeling dejected, Lara surprises her privately, answering her inquiry with a kiss. Lacey has launched a "Stop the Menace" campaign against Shane, stalking her on the streets and publicly shaming her at The Planet for committing the four Fs: "finds 'em, feels 'em, fucks 'em, and forgets 'em." And Tim decides to throw a last-minute dinner party to celebrate his engagement to Jenny, bringing together his friends Randy Jackson (Kwesi Ameyaw) and Carolyn Varajian (Jennifer Copping) with neighbors Bette and Tina and, much to Jenny's surprise and dismay, Marina. Her presence at their table unsettles Jenny as she tries to balance the weight of her new engagement ring with the judgment she senses from Marina, who is watching her carefully if discreetly. But Marina isn't the only one who has her eye on Jenny: Bette witnesses an emotionally intimate exchange between the two women in the kitchen, setting off her self-righteous temper and compelling her to confront Marina in Tim and Jenny's bathroom before making an abrupt exit from the dinner party.

Lara Perkins, played by Lauren Lee Smith

Best known as the "soup chef," Lara Perkins is the sous chef at Dana Fairbanks's tennis club and becomes her first serious girlfriend. Dana feels torn, with Lara trying to pull her out of the closet and her agent Conrad shoving her back in. Out of fear, she breaks up with Lara, worried that being out will ruin her career. Lara reappears in the second season when Kit hires her as The Planet's new chef. Lara is excited to see the out, loud, and proud Dana, who is now involved with Alice. She can't resist inviting Dana to dinner, and though she's never been the home-wrecking type, Lara is finding it hard to discourage her ex's flirtations. After all, their relationship ended just when the going was good.

Lauren Lee Smith appeared in the television miniseries *Christy: Choices of the Heart,* and in the television series *Mutant X, The Dead Zone,* and *Dark Angel,* among others. She is in Tony Goldwyn's forthcoming film *The Last Kiss,* costarring with Zach Braff, Blythe Danner, and Casey Affleck. Lauren Smith admits, "I can't cook—not for the life of me. I've been spoiled rotten by my mother, who is a phenomenal cook. Those scenes where I cut my finger . . . our catering services showed me how to chop. I practiced for so long for one little shot."

"Longing": Episode 104
Written by Angela Robinson
Directed by Lynne Stopkewich

No sooner does Alice end up in bed with Gabby than Gabby's back to all her old playa tricks. Bette, Tina, Dana, and Shane plead with Alice to get some self-respect and dump her, even suggesting a few choice lines to use. Dana has her first date with Lara, and Shane finally puts an end to Lacey's "4-F" campaign—now with flyers and banners—by indulging her obsessive angst with a mercy fuck. Tim drops by The Planet and plays pool with Marina, the sight of which causes an undernourished Jenny to pass out and then later project her guilt onto him when she accuses him of flirting with the Italian temptress. Bette

also has a fainting spell, which happens in the hotel room of Peggy Peabody, a steel heiress and a major art collector and benefactor. Bette goes to visit her in a desperate plea to save her job at the CAC by persuading Peggy to let her have the controversial show "Provocations"—she has already canceled the CAC perennial bore, "Impressions in Winter," which her boss, Franklin Phillips, booked behind her back. When Peggy shows her a life-size portrait by Bette's favorite photographer, Carla Marie Freed, she swoons, forever winning Peggy's affection.

This Is the Episode in Which . . .

• Bette tells Peggy Peabody that she is a "has-bian," after the steel heiress confesses to being a lesbian for a year, in 1974.

• Tina tries to reach out to Jenny and tells her that the lesbian community is a "hotbed of rumor and innuendo," cluing her in to the fact that her affair with Marina is obvious to anyone with eyesight.

• Jenny confronts Marina in her office, telling her: "Every time I look at you, I feel so completely dismantled." Jenny looks as if she's about to lose her grip but instead loses the sweatshirt and discovers the pleasures of vertical sex with Marina.

Music featured in this episode:

"Revolution," Fundamental

"Borrito," Fundamental

Alice sings her version of "Mickey," Toni Basil

"Rack 'Em," Dan Gagnon

"Celly Q," Dan Gagnon

"Blinded," Dan Gagnon

"Discovered," Kinnie Starr

"At the Speed of Light," Transientworld

"Soaring," Schumann

"Where, 2?" Chris Gestrin Trio

"Slowly," Joystick

"Right in Time," Lucinda Williams

L Is for . . . Linking It Up

In season one, beginning with this episode, the show opens with a cryptic erotic vignette which the creators refer to as a "Random Sex Act." The Acts often set the tone for the episode. Some of them have an obvious connection to the story line, while others have a more elusive link. Let's see just how random they are:

Title Card: New York City, 1986

Carla Marie Freed is snapping photographs in a dark studio of a nude woman standing completely still, her face looking straight ahead, her hands turned out. She appears illuminated and almost Christlike. The photographer approaches the subject and begins to kiss her.

The Link-up

Art collector Peggy Peabody has bought this photo on a spending spree. She shows the life-size portrait to Bette, who faints at the sight of it and experiences Stendhal syndrome, a psychosomatic illness that borrows its name from the nineteenth-century French author. Stendhal had a similar spell in 1817, on seeing a painting by Caravaggio; he described the episode in his book *Naples and Florence: A Journey from Milan to Reggio.* Both Bette and Peggy love the work of Carla Marie Freed, who died of a drug overdose. This bond saves Bette's job at the CAC.

Peggy Peabody, played by Holland Taylor

The heiress of United Steel and an extremely wealthy if eccentric art collector and benefactor, Peggy Peabody becomes an indispensable ally to Bette Porter when she helps to bring the "Provocations" show to the CAC and keeps the board of directors from canceling Bette's contract. Peggy's retirement from the Peabody Foundation threatens Bette's position at the CAC, in part because their bond is a source of envy for Peggy's daughter, Helena, who now runs the foundation.

Holland Taylor is an Emmy-winning comic actress who has appeared in innumerable films, such as *Legally Blonde, The Truman Show,* and *To Die For,* and television programs, including *Monk, The Practice,* and *Veronica's Closet.* She currently appears on *Two and a Half Men,* which earned her another Emmy nomination.

Jennifer Beals on Holland Taylor:

"I just watch Holland in this scene, and I think, I'm getting schooled in how to use props right now. It's fascinating to watch how beautifully she used everything in the room."

Franklin Phillips, played by Michael Tomlinson

The chairman of the CAC board of directors, Franklin is Bette Porter's cautious boss, who hires her to shake things up and raise the museum's profile but can't stomach the controversy that comes with provocative exhibitions. His hand-wringing cowardice will ultimately cost Bette her job.

Michael Tomlinson has appeared in a number of television shows, including *The Shield, Resurrection Blvd., JAG,* and *The West Wing.*

"Lies, Lies, Lies": Episode 105

Written by Josh Senter
Directed by Clement Virgo

Tim is on edge when Jenny's predatory writing mentor, Nick Barashkov, comes to town. Jenny excitedly tells Nick how she killed off her fictional alter ego, Sarah Schuster; still, her latest work bores him, but not her adventures with Marina. Dana flees her own apartment out of embarrassment when she should be enjoying her first afterglow with Lara, mistaking her rare ability to ejaculate for bed-wetting. After the Gabby Deveaux debacle, Alice swears off women, and

This Is the Episode in Which . . .

- Alice tells Tina, "I could use a little nice, uncomplicated, boring, boy-girl sex masquerading as love."

- Jenny first starts disconnecting during sex with Tim.

- Tim almost catches Marina and Jenny getting it on at The Planet—twice.

- Shane and Lenore share a kiss at Bette and Tina's poolside.

- We meet Dana's beloved cat, Mr. Piddles, for the first time.

Lenore Pieszecki, played by Anne Archer

Alice's mother, Lenore, is an ebullient has-been-never-quite-was Hollywood actress who loves to tell stories and embellish them to the max. She has been keeping the flame alive on her short flicker of fame for decades. But her delusions of grandeur are beginning to cost Alice a lot of money, as she bails Lenore out of one luxury hotel after another.

A Golden Globe winner for her role in *Short Cuts,* Anne Archer has appeared in countless films since, though she probably is best known for her Oscar-nominated turn as Michael Douglas's wife in Adrian Lyne's *Fatal Attraction.*

Lisa, played by Devon Gummersall

Lisa is the lesbian-identified man whom Shane introduces to Alice soon after she swears off "the drama and mind-fucks" of being with women. He may have a gentle disposition and a unique talent for administering Reiki via telepathy, but it puzzles Alice that he of the manly body would insist on making love to her with a dildo. And he is smothering her more than any female lesbian she's ever met!

Perhaps best known for his role as the lovably nerdy Brian Krakow on *My So-Called Life,* Devon Gummersall has appeared in the films *Reeker, The Young Unknowns,* and *It's My Party,* and the television programs *Without a Trace, Monk, Roswell, Felicity,* and *Relativity,* among many others.

L Is for . . . Linking It Up

Title Card: Greenwich Village, Present Day

Two women are sleeping in bed. The camera pans over a small array of ancient demon statuettes on a table. Someone bangs on the door. A woman named Tess puts on her clothes and goes to answer it, almost knocking over the statuette of Abraxas, the demon of deceit. She is holding it in her hand when she opens the door to see her friend Helen, who is panicked because her girlfriend, Stacy, never came home the night before. Tess assures Helen that her girlfriend is probably fine, and returns to bed, and into the arms of Stacy.

The Link-up

Jenny's writing mentor, Nick Barashkov, is coming to town. They once had an affair, presumably before she and Tim were together. Tim is mistrustful of him because he encourages Jenny to explore her dark side. Tim recognizes that he doesn't trust Jenny, but he's not sure why. When her dinner with Nick runs late, Tim turns up at Nick's hotel room expecting to find them in a compromising position. The deception, of course, is happening at The Planet, in Marina's back office. Later, Jenny writes about Abraxas while everyone is celebrating Tina's pregnancy in their backyard. And Stacy and Tess turn up in "L'Ennui," at Shane's fabulous yacht party, splashing around naked in the pool.

Nick Barashkov, played by Julian Sands

Nick Barashkov is Jenny Schecter's dandyish, slightly sinister writing professor from the University of Chicago. He and Jenny had an affair years earlier, which is one reason why Tim can't stand him. The other is that Nick likes to taunt Tim and encourage Jenny to explore her macabre psyche.

British leading man Julian Sands first captured the attention of American audiences with his role in James Ivory's film adaptation of *A Room with a View.* Since then, he's been in a number of films, among them *The Million Dollar Hotel, Leaving Las Vegas,* and *Impromptu.*

Music featured in this episode:

"Lady Love," Joystick

"Pacific Theme," Broken Social Scene

"Husband and Wife," Patric Caird

"Organic," Fundamental

"Last Night," Paloma

"Microphone," Transientworld

"I'm Gonna be the One," Sattalites

"Clouds on Ground," Hellenkeller

"My Secret Life," Leonard Cohen

switch hits over to men as a way of simplifying her love life. Then she gets a crush on Lisa, a "lesbian-identified man." Could he be the best of both worlds, or her worst nightmare? Tina's early pregnancy test delivers good news, which she shares with Alice, who proves incapable of keeping a secret. Bette hates being the last to know, but seizing her attention is near impossible. It turns out that canceling the previously scheduled shows without officially securing "Provocations"—a show no one at the CAC is embracing—has not exactly endeared Bette to Franklin, who is about to cut her loose. It's a good thing Peggy Peabody is still in town to bail her out. Alice's mom, Lenore, also needs to be bailed out, from a huge debt she's racked up at the Plaza Hotel. Alice grows increasingly suspicious of her actress mother's Hollywood tales when she spies Lenore at a general casting call for a low-rent horror movie director, even as she claims to be in town to star in the new Gerard Lichtman film.

"Lawfully": Episode 106
Written by Rose Troche
Directed by Daniel Minahan

Everyone is in for a rude awakening: Marina tells Jenny that her writing isn't perfect. Dana is in love's thrall, but her agent tries to squelch it when he puts the kibosh on her public displays of affection with Lara and instructs the up-and-comer to straighten her image by bringing Harrison to a Subaru dinner in the interest of securing the endorsement deal. Bette eagerly awaits the visit of her father, Dr. Melvin Porter, so she can share the news of Tina's pregnancy, despite the fact he's barely acknowledged Tina's existence during their seven-year relationship. Kit is perplexed by Bette's shock and devastation when Melvin, a man who has always cleaved to conservative values, coldly rejects the notion that Bette and Tina's baby could be his future grandchild. But Kit goes to see Melvin to speak on Bette's behalf, warn-

This Is the Episode in Which . . .

- Alice unloads Lenore on her brother, Nelson, after Lenore tries to put her name on the Chart.

- Bette and Tina discuss the possibility of merging their last names for the sake of the baby. Bette suggests, "Portard."

- Lara gently demands that Dana take steps toward coming out.

- Kit gets a note from her estranged son, David, requesting his medical history.

L Is for . . . Linking It Up

Title Card: West Hollywood, California, 1976

A man, Sammy, shoves a man, Stephen, against the wall of a diner bathroom. Stephen tries to kiss Sammy, who pushes him away and moves to the other side of the room. He unbuckles and unzips his pants, and says to Stephen, "You ready? I bet you are." Stephen walks over and tries to kiss him again, but Sammy directs his face downward, and moans with disgusted pleasure. The next shot is of Sammy pulling Stephen out of the bathroom and into a busy dining area, flashing his badge, and yelling, "Stephen Green, you fuckin' faggot, you have the right to remain silent. Anything you say can and will be used against you."

The Link-up

A sheriff stops Tim for speeding as he races back from ditching Jenny in Tahoe. Why, it's Sammy. Tim finds a sympathetic ear in this sheriff and spills his guts. But he's sorry that he did, because Sammy gives him a creepy earload about homosexuality, sharing this theory: "When you got two people, they got the same equipment, and they both know how to treat it. How could anybody of the opposite sex compete with that? That's how they get ya." And we know that he speaks from experience.

ing her father that he will lose his daughter if he denies her his blessing. And proving that the third time's the charm, Tim finally catches Marina and Jenny in the act. Jenny claims it was a one-off and begs Tim not to leave her. Absolution comes at a price: Tim makes Jenny tell Marina she's made a "terrible mistake," that "it will never happen again," and that she will never see her again. The unhappy couple elopes to Lake Tahoe, but Tim feels empty and abandons Jenny there the morning after their wedding. At The Planet, Shane runs into hustler Clive (Matthew Currie Holmes), an old colleague from her bygone days of selling handjobs on Santa Monica Boulevard, when she passed for a guy. Clive is now the boy toy of Hollywood's Velvet Mafia and eager for a time-out.

Music featured in this episode:

"Everybody's Somebody's Fool," Connie Francis

"Ran Kan Kan," Latin Dance Project

"Wish You Well," Bet.e and Stef

"Remix," Fundamental

"Edge," Mark Petersen

"October Rain," 5 Alarm

"A Bit of Bubbly," 5 Alarm

"Coco Love," Dan Gagnon

"Rock Machine," Copyright

"People Ain't No Good," Nick Cave

Melvin Porter, played by Ossie Davis

A physician who considers himself a self-made, God-fearing man, Melvin Porter is the father of Kit and Bette. Kit harbors resentment toward her father because her African-American mother put Melvin through medical school, only to be abandoned for the white woman who would become Bette's mother. Melvin has little patience for Kit, who has struggled with drugs, alcohol, and bad choices in men and business. He adores Bette, a Yale graduate and successful art curator who has inherited his temperament and sense of pride, but he is convinced she is going to have to answer to God for her lesbianism. Both of his daughters care for him as he dies of advanced prostate cancer, and though the three grant each other resolution and absolution, he leaves this earth with a few lingering questions.

An award-winning actor, director, writer, and producer, Ossie Davis, with his wife, Ruby Dee, was one of the finest, most prolific, and highly praised artists of his generation. He and Ruby Dee were also civil rights activists: Ossie delivered eulogies at the funerals of both Malcolm X and Martin Luther King, Jr. Ossie and Ruby Dee were honored at the Kennedy Center in 2004. He passed away at age eighty-seven on February 4, 2005.

Jennifer Beals says:

"He was truly an exemplary human being. I just feel so fortunate to have been, in some infinitesimal way, a part of his trajectory, to have been in his company, and to have seen him and Ruby together, because they were so in love—my God! The way they'd look at each other across the room, it was just so, so beautiful. He was really such a gentleman, and so funny and so smart and so eloquent."

Pam Grier says:

"He had the immense strength to live out his life in the arts. His passion to play Melvin so brilliantly—he brought forth something that would help the African-American community to see this man that was such a pillar for what he had done for black theater, for the community, for civil rights. The fact that Ossie brought such strength and power—you want that bloodcurdling, vessel-splitting energy that you could respond to, and he brought that. That's the generosity of a fine actor that you hope to work with."

"Losing It": Episode 107
Written by Guinevere Turner
Directed by Clement Virgo

Tim's guilt over abandoning a penniless Jenny in Tahoe turns to rage when Bette inadvertently reveals that the affair was going on for at least a month. Tim goes to The Planet to confront Marina, and gloves are off when she refuses to express remorse. In the meantime, a tearstained Jenny has hitched a ride with an SUV full of teenagers who give her 'shrooms and spends the long drive home writing an overwrought letter to Tim offering up her internal organs, and alternately crying her eyes out and tripping her face off. Bette heads to the "Provocations" opening at MoMA in New York at the personal invitation of Peggy Peabody, regretfully leaving a nauseated Tina at home. Tina goes to see a Chinese herbalist for relief, and instead gets an earload of grief from a harrowing encounter in the waiting room with Marcus Allenwood's shrill girlfriend, Lei Ling (Taayla Markell), who bar-

This Is the Episode in Which . . .

- Shane's roommates plan the Twat: The Night party at The Planet.

- Bette gains a reputation in New York for being "the sister that snatched the [Provocations] show from under MoCA's nose."

- Kit reads the girls at the poker game for making fun of Lisa's decision to be a lesbian:

"What is it with you people and your need to take apart everything and process each little detail? If the dude wanna give up his white-man rights to be a second-class citizen, then, hey, welcome to our world."

- Dana and Lara get caught finger-banging at the slumber party.

106

rages Tina's answering machine with menacing messages threatening to sue her and Bette for custody of the unborn child. Tina is wigged and tries to reach Bette in New York, leaving several teary, incoherent voicemails. But Bette can't reach her when the gang—Shane, Kit, Dana, Lara, Alice, and Lisa—convince Tina to unplug the phone for the duration of their sleepover poker game. Fearing the worst, a terrified Bette hops the first plane back to LA, missing the dinner Peggy threw expressly for her. Gay real estate mogul Harry Samchuk (Colin Cunningham) is at once gobsmacked and impressed when he learns that Shane is female; in a gesture of goodwill, he shoves a bullet full of Oxy up her nose at a nightclub, and by morning, sends over her first A-list client: Ellie Zimmer, "studio chiefess, trend priestess, friend of Madonna and J. Lo, both at the same time," according to Shane's sycophantic boss at Lather, the hair salon where she works.

Music featured in this episode:

"I Don't Want U," Widelife

"Sunday Funk," Earthmen

"Buttergroove," Fundamental

"All Suns 1," Beans

"Venus," Metalwood

"Ooh Boy," Joystick

"Pastures of Heaven," Ridley Bent

"Dreaming," Kinnie Starr

"See Through You," Flunk

"In Spite of All the Damage," Be Good Tanyas

L Is for . . . Linking It Up

Title Card: Detroit, Michigan, Two Years Ago

It is after hours at Marsie & Chick's Sub Shop, and two teenaged girls are chatting and halfheartedly cleaning up. Their manager comes in and yells, "You got time to lean, you got time to clean!" One girl picks up a broom and makes a sweeping motion until he leaves. "What a tool," she says, and then walks over to her friend Katie and the two begin making out. The boss stomps toward the back room to check on them and finds them locking lips. He whips out his dick and starts stroking.

The Link-up

When Jenny hitchhikes back from Tahoe, her teenaged driver regales her with a tragic version of this story, in which one of the girls kills herself. Another passenger announces it was only an afterschool special.

"L'Ennui": Episode 108
Written by Ilene Chaiken
Directed by Tony Goldwyn

Agrimy Jenny makes her way back to West Hollywood, with pleas for forgiveness: Tim gives the dirty girl a chance to come clean, but when she lies again by insisting that what happened with Marina was a one-night stand, he puts her out on the street. So Jenny turns up at The Planet to ask Marina to please forget her whole terrible-mistake/never-see-her-again spiel. Because Marina is more forgiving, Jenny finagles a bath and a sleepover, too. But when she asks to stay the week, Marina surprises her with news of the existence of a girlfriend, costume designer Francesca Wolff, who's about to return from Europe. Alice, Shane, and Dana are concerned about Bette and Tina, who have become so

This Is the Episode in Which...

• Alice, Dana, and Shane administer a multiple-choice self-assessment test to Bette and Tina to demonstrate to them how boring they've become since Tina got pregnant.

• Dana first sees the mock-up of the Subaru ad with its motto: "Get Out and Stay Out."

• Jenny and Marina go to Shane's yacht party together—their first public date.

• Dana debuts her now-famous drunken boat dance.

• In a rare moment of candor, Shane reveals a desire to settle down when she admiringly confesses,

"I've been thinking about it. What's more boring, right? You can make endless lists. You can bawl your head off and puke over the side of the boat. Or you get to go home. You get to sleep with the same person you've been in love with for seven years."

• Kit diagnoses Bette's mounting anxiety as "the daddy blues," because she is "worrying about all the responsibilities coming down . . . the financial responsibilities, the 'I-can't-take-any-more-risks' responsibilities. 'Cause now there are two other lives that are totally dependent on you keeping everything together."

• Tim slowly lets Jenny insinuate herself back into his house.

L Is for . . . Linking It Up

Title Card: Rome, Italy, Present Day

A beautiful Italian woman is standing on a platform. A costume designer is kneeling beside her, fitting her into a beautiful gown, telling her about her last job, a film version of *The Gift of the Magi*. The woman isn't familiar with the story. The designer recounts it for her, while sliding her hand under the dress and up her leg, arousing the young woman with both the story and the movement of her hand.

The Link-up

This is our informal introduction to Marina Ferrer's lover, Francesca Wolff. Jenny will learn about her in this episode, but she won't meet her until "Listen Up."

Music featured in this episode:

"Connais-Tu Le Pays?" Ultimate Opera

"Un Año de Amor," Luz Casal

"It's Alright Now," Mercury Sound Cartel

"A Very Cellular Song," Mike Heron

"Bittersweet Love," Mercury Sound Cartel

"Love Can't Wait," Moka Only

"Legal," Snow

"Bahia Clouds," Mercury Sound Cartel

"Mambo Lupita," Latin Dance

"O Oh No Oh," Monkey Boys

"Hands Up," Kia Kadiri

"Seven," Bob Beals

"Chameleon," Transientworld

"Alright," Kinnie Starr

"In Time," Patric Caird

"R7 Jazz," Patric Caird

"Those Three Days," Lucinda Williams

dreadfully boring in their domestic revelry that the trio feel they must stage an intervention, but they don't do it in time to get out of attending a Sikh chanting ceremony. Kit's son, David Waters (Colin Lawrence), asks to meet her at his hotel but leaves when he thinks he sees her having a drink at the bar. Dana's agent continues to misadvise her about hiding her sexuality when he warns her of the "Lifestyle Clause." It turns out Subaru wants to make her a "gay Anna Kournikova," which ultimately costs her agent his job, but not before Dana reluctantly breaks up with Lara, who has been increasingly pressuring her to come out. Everyone shows up at Shane's knock-down-drag-out girlie party on Harry's yacht, even Bette and Tina. Dana tries to numb her heartache with alcohol but instead drinks herself sick. And in a private cabin, Lisa and Alice are finally getting down to business after so many back rubs. But then he grabs for a dildo, insisting on making love to Alice like a lesbian. When Alice demands that Lisa fuck her like the man he is, he acts as if she violated him.

Francesca Wolff, played by Lolita Davidovich

Costume designer Francesca Wolff is Marina Ferrer's lover and the financier of all her whims, including The Planet. Francesca and Marina have an open relationship when Francesca is away on jobs, which is most of the year, since her work on films and international ballets takes her all over the world. But when she comes home, she requires Marina's fullest attention.

Lolita Davidovich has been in a number of films, including *Jake's Women, Gods and Monsters,* and *Blaze,* and has guest-starred on *The Agency, Monk,* and *CSI: Crime Scene Investigation.*

"Listen Up": Episode 109
Written by Mark Zakarin
Directed by Kari Skogland

Tim is away, so Jenny has invited old college pal Annette Bishop (Sarah Strange)—reluctant real estate broker by day, riotous rocker by night—to play. As Jenny regales Annette with the sordid details of her recent life, she begins to consider her sexual identity for the first time, while Annette plots their Francesca Wolff–assessment mission. The Subaru ad is starting to appear in national magazines, and Dana is in a full-blown panic. She has to tell her Republican parents before someone else does. Alice accompanies her to the Orange County Republican Women's Coalition luncheon, with the plan to get Dana to tell Mrs. Fairbanks just before she receives her Woman of the Year Award. But it doesn't play out as neatly as all that, and the family's reaction puts a new spin on "Get Out and Stay Out." No sooner does Tina drag Bette to Dan Foxworthy's expectant parents' therapy group than Bette gets into a brawl over identity politics with a self-righteous African-American lesbian poet

Music featured in this episode:

"Crimson and Clover," Tommy James and the Shondells

"Why Ask Why," Hissy Fit

"Blue Sky," Jason Collett

"Sub Zero," 5 Alarm

"Revolution," Fundamental

"Love Is My Middle Name," Joystick

"Flutter," Bonobo

"Camel Toe," Stinkmitt

"Foolish Love," Rufus Wainwright

This Is the Episode in Which . . .

- Jenny admits to her college friend Annette that Marina is as hot as she is humorless.

- We meet Dana's bratty younger brother, Howie, who taunts her about the Subaru ad and jokingly promises her, "When Mom and Dad disown you and all, I'll still come and visit"—a promise he makes good on in "Loud and Proud."

- Jenny marvels at Francesca's sophistication:

"She's like Belmondo, in, like, this Godard film. You know? I live out of a garbage bag. I live in a toolshed."

- Clive lays a guilt trip on Shane when she initially refuses to give him money and drugs:

"You know, the reason you have this money is because of me. I mean, I'm the one who got you where you are. All right. I'm the one who set you up. If it wasn't for me you never would have met Harry and you never would have had any clients! You owe me!"

- Shane theorizes about Sharon Fairbanks's negative reaction to Dana coming out.

"It probably means at some point she fell in love with one of her friends and got her heart broken."

- During group therapy, Bette wonders to herself,

"Am I just panicking? Is this about the baby? Or am I falling out of love?"

Sharon and Irwin Fairbanks, played by Susan and Michael Hogan

Dana's Republican parents love their daughter, but her lesbianism is hard for them to accept, especially for Sharon, who struggled with her own lesbian desires when she was younger.

The Hogans are married in real life. Susan has appeared on *The Outer Limits*, *Poltergeist: The Legacy*, *Dark Angel,* and other programs. Michael has a recurring role on *Battlestar Galactica* and has most recently appeared on *Monk* and *The Outer Limits*.

named Yolanda Watkins (Kim Hawthorne). Bette could use the batting practice, because some conservative Christians are starting to harass her and the CAC about the upcoming "Provocations" show. Kit revels in the flattery of having hip-hop star Slim Daddy request permission to sample her 1986 hit "It's the Real Thing" and have her star in his video. As Kit gets ready to sign on the dotted line, Bette eyeballs the offer—a measly $1,000, no royalties—and suggests Kit get a lawyer. It's the condescending tone that kills the joy for Kit, not the advice itself. Shane spies Clive rummaging through her roommate's unattended bag at The Planet. It turns out he's been filching other things, too, so she kicks him out, whereupon he returns to tricking on their old stomping ground. The night brings the Twat party at a nearby nightclub, where attendees must enter through a gigantic faux labia majora. Annette poses as Jenny's girlfriend to vex Marina. But it is Jenny who becomes unsettled, when the cunning Francesca introduces herself and invites the young writer over to their house for dinner.

Slim Daddy, played by Snoop Dogg

Slim Daddy is a charming, flirty hip-hop artist who samples Kit's 1986 hit song "It's the Real Thing" on his latest album and offers to choreograph a video around the legendary R&B star. Slim takes a shine to Bette and encourages her to get together with Candace, whom she meets at one of Kit's gigs.

Snoop Dogg, a.k.a. Calvin Broadus, is an enduring multiplatinum LA-based hip-hop artist and a talented comic actor, who has turned up in such movies as *Starsky & Hutch*, *Soul Plane*, and *Half-Baked*.

L Is for . . . Linking It Up

Title Card: Santa Rosa, California, 1968

Two young women, Leslie and Sharon, are at the horse stables bemoaning the fact that they won't get to spend the summer together and speaking wistfully about how much they will miss each other. They hug, and Sharon starts kissing Leslie on the mouth. Leslie pushes her away in disgust and says, "People have all kinds of feelings. It doesn't mean we're supposed to act on them!"

The Link-up

The young Sharon turns out to be Dana's mother as a teenager. Maybe that's why Mrs. Fairbanks, a lifelong Republican, takes it so badly when Dana comes out to her at a banquet in her honor. Sharon rebukes Dana, with the exact humiliating words Leslie used on her more than thirty years earlier.

"Luck, Next Time": Episode 110

Written by Rose Troche
Directed by Rose Troche

Bette's ambivalent thoughts might be confined to the privacy of her head, but Tina can sense her pulling away. Then Tina miscarries their baby, and Bette's confusion is compounded by grief. After breaking up with Lara and coming out to her parents, Dana is convinced that she has earned the scorn of the whole world. Alice, who has had enough of Dana's pity party bed-in, gets mother and daughter talking again, but unfortunately it results in Sharon Fairbanks fixing Dana up on a blind date with a guy. All is not lost for said straight boy: After Dana tells him she's

This Is the Episode in Which . . .

• We see that Marina is beholden to and resentful of Francesca.

• Dana comes out to Mr. Piddles, her cat.

• The morning after they sleep together, Tim tells Jenny,

"I don't wanna be back together with you, Jenny. I mean, I don't know who you are. I mean, you just start talking about Marina and her girlfriend and how phony and manipulative they are and all I can think is, that's you! That's who you've become. It's like you've done this thing and you can't wash it off."

• Steve Jaffe creepily tells Shane that she has a talent for making his wife look hot.

"I thought I was gonna bang her right there. You know how many men think that about their own wives? None. You could be a gold mine, you know that?"

James, played by Preston Cook

James is Bette Porter's loyal if put-upon assistant at the CAC. He's adept at the usual tasks—scheduling appointments, answering her phone, Googling, personal shopping. But he is most treasured by Bette for his protective skills, guarding her from Franklin, Faye Buckley, Leo Herrera, Helena Peabody, and any other interloper who might stand in her way. He begins to falter when Helena takes a more active role at the CAC and threatens his job.

Preston Cook has appeared on *Stargate SG-1*, *The 4400*, and *The Twilight Zone*, among other television series.

Music featured in this episode:

"Sol Ja Camba," Fantcha

"True Soul," Kia Kadiri

"Tomorrowland," Mercury Sound Cartel

"It's the Real Thing," Pam Grier

"Lose Yourself," Mercury Sound Cartel

"Greatest Gift," Coco Love Alcorn

"Mirror," by French Suspense

"Seasons," Mercury Sound Cartel

"Why?" Fundamental

"Sol's Favrit Beat," Social Deviantz

"Blinded," Dan Gagnon

"Good Times," Joystick

"Into My Arms," Nick Cave

gay, Alice hits on him to escape from Lisa, who is suffocating her with his lezzie codependent shtick. The veritable CEO of Hollywood wives, Cherie Jaffe, comes into Lather for her first haircut with Shane and enjoys it so much that she summons her for a house call. Only this time, Cherie has other services she wants rendered. Thankfully, Shane is fast on her clunky boots, because Mr. Jaffe (James Purcell) doesn't believe in knocking before entering and almost catches them in the act. Marina and Francesca have Jenny for dinner, or so it feels to her. She misinterprets Marina's pained, sulky expression as icy detachment, and when the insecure Francesca boasts of her conquests abroad and implies that Marina has done the same by sharing every intimate detail with her, Jenny flees in disgust. But not before taking the bottle of wine she brought—snubbed by Miss "Gifts of the Vagi"—and shattering it against their glass house. She returns home to an impromptu invite by Tim to watch kung fu movies. Couch snuggles quickly devolve into a night of belated breakup sex that leaves Tim with a bad hangover. Slim Daddy flirts with Bette as she watches Kit on his video shoot and asks her to return with all of her lady friends when the video is reshot to work in a hoochie-lesbo-

L Is for . . . Linking It Up

Title Card: Lisbon, Portugal, Present Day

Latin guitar music plays as the camera takes us through an exquisite house, up the stairs to the balcony, where we finally see a Jesus-like figure, his hands outstretched, the wall illuminated behind him. He is flanked by three old wise men. The vision of the four men is totally still, as if they are posing for a painting. A woman comes in. It is the artist Isabella Pernao. The camera moves, and we can't see her. When we see her again, she is on all fours doggie-style in front of the Jesus figure, rocking back and forth as if she is getting off on him. He is unmoved, and her face betrays no emotion. The camera pulls back and we see a video tripod capturing the scenario.

The Link-up

This very piece is the lightning rod of the "Provocations" show. Isabella Pernao's work has attracted the attention of zealot Faye Buckley and her conservative organization Coalition for Concerned Citizens, who are protesting the forthcoming exhibit and trying to prevent her work from entering the CAC by any means necessary.

Cherie Jaffe, played by Rosanna Arquette

The CEO of Hollywood-mogul wives, Cherie Jaffe is the sexy older woman who opens Shane's heart to love. But when Cherie mistakenly believes that Shane hooked up with her daughter, she coldly dumps her, leading Shane to think that love isn't worth the pain.

The Emmy-nominated, BAFTA Award–winning actress Rosanna Arquette has been acting in films since she was a teenager. Her movies include *Big Bad Love, Things Behind the Sun, Pulp Fiction,* and *Desperately Seeking Susan.* In 2002, she made her directorial debut with *Searching for Debra Winger.* Katherine Moennig says, "Rosanna Arquette just goes for it every time. She is balls to the wall. She's fantastic!"

chic angle. A bit of Googling leads CAC assistant James to link a name with the creepy phone calls and mysterious flowers being delivered to Bette: Faye Buckley and her Coalition for Concerned Citizens, who have been following "Provocations" around the country, and all the way onto Bette and Tina's front lawn. Faye personally ensures that Bette has received her gifts when she engages her in an eerie exchange outside the CAC and has it secretly filmed.

"Liberally": Episode 111
Written by Ilene Chaiken
Directed by Mary Harron

Music featured in this episode:

"Flower," Liz Phair

"Fish n Chips," Hellenkeller

"Gloria's Song," Family Man

"New Foundation," Kia Kadiri

"Good Foot," Kia Kadiri

"Canción de la Paloma," Paloma

"Never Say Goodbye," Pam Grier

"Nu Deli," Meta 4

"Abilene," Bottleneck

"Drivin' You," Auburn

"Aerial Dust," Transientworld

"Quiza, Quiza, Quiza," Mariachi Los Camperos de Nati Cano

"No Me Quieras Tanto," Mariachi Los Camperos de Nati Cano

"Hallelujah," Rufus Wainwright

Since Tina's miscarriage, Bette has been working more furiously than ever. In addition to "Provocations," she has another show to put on: a televised face-off with Faye Buckley, who manipulated the footage of their CAC confrontation for a propaganda video that was sent to every conservative congressman in the nation. Reeling from grief, Tina can barely get herself out of the house except to attend Dan Foxworthy's therapy group. One of the group members, Oscar (Zak Santiago), suggests she channel her sorrow into volunteer work at his office, the Headquarters for Social Justice. When Tina arrives the following day, she requests a project that will help Bette: a Faye Buckley fact-finding mission. She and Oscar hit paydirt—and, boy, is it dirty. At Lather, Shane glams up Dana with a fabulous makeover, while Alice blows them away with news that Lisa might have gotten her

L Is for . . . Linking It Up

Title card: San Fernando Valley, Last Year

Two teenaged girls in Catholic schoolgirl outfits, China and Amber, are applying makeup in a school bathroom mirror. The camera pulls back to reveal movie cameras, microphones, and men. When the director yells, "Bring in the pussy light!" it's clear that this is a porn set. The filming begins, and the girls start unbuttoning their shirts and kissing each other before China starts working her way down Amber's body. The "principal" storms in and catches the girls, who pretend to be surprised and then segue into mock arousal. China walks over to the principal, unzips his pants, and blows him. The director orders the principal to "pop on her face, give her a facial," and China is instructed to say, "That was great."

The Link-up

Tina's friends at the Headquarters for Social Justice turn up quality dirt on Faye Buckley in time for Bette's television debate with her on *Insight*. Faye's daughter, Cora, was being abused by her father, and Faye did nothing to stop it. Cora ran away when she was fourteen, and Faye paid off a district court judge to have the police records expunged. Cora is none other than China from *Here Cums the Principal*.

This Is the Episode in Which . . .

- Alice grosses out Shane and Dana in equal amounts with tales of her heterosexual exploits with a real straight guy.

- Bette meets Candace Jewell, the ex-girlfriend of Bette's group therapy nemesis, at Kit's show. Slim Daddy tells Bette, "I think the two of you would, uh, you know, yeah. Lord have mercy on me."

- Clea Jaffe tries to make a pass at Shane and is gently rebuffed.

- Tim and his top swimmer, Trish Peverell, begin an illicit affair, which Jenny threatens to report to Randy.

pregnant. There's only one karmically sound thing to do with the first "lesbian-to-lesbian" conception, according to Shane: Give the baby to Bette and Tina. Marina can hardly stand Francesca, whose money, we learn, keeps The Planet rotating. Shane is walking on air when Cherie gives her a couple of choice sneak peeks: the first, a glimpse of the salon space her husband has picked out for her; the other, a vision of herself ready and waiting on a barbershop chair. So when Steve Jaffe pawns their troubled gay daughter, Clea (Samantha McLeod), off on her for the day, Shane has no choice but to comply. Jenny braves a solo outing to LA's oldest lesbian bar and runs into Dana, whom she brings back to her studio. Their lack of chemistry is as palpable as their loneliness, so they give sex a few disastrously awkward attempts, but have the sense to stop it before anyone gets injured. At the debate, when Bette confronts her with her daughter's porn video, Faye shocks even herself with the depths to which she will sink to win a debate, declaring that Bette and Tina's daughter died because God was protecting her from living in sin.

"Looking Back": Episode 112

Written by Guinevere Turner
Directed by Rose Troche

Fresh out of the closet, Dana is already collecting awards for her courage: She road-trips to Palm Springs for the Kraft-Nabisco Professional Women's Golf Tournament—a.k.a. the Dinah Shore Weekend—to accept a Human Rights Campaign (HRC) award, and takes Alice, Shane, Tina, and Jenny with her. Lenore wangles a lift home from the girls, but it means bearing a rousing, off-key, and interminable singalong of the Indigo Girls' "Closer to Fine." Lenore stops it the only way she knows how: by embarrassing her poor daughter. She regales the troops with her version of Alice's coming-out story, which involves a cute drunken high school grope session and vomiting where the kissing should have been. Alice corrects Lenore: Her first love was Tayo (Marta Jaciubek), the bass player in her college punk-rock band. Then everyone else contributes their stories: Dana recounts the tale she referenced in the pilot, about falling in love with a now-famous tennis player, once her tennis camp counselor, whom she calls "Ralph" (Tara Wilson) to protect her identity. Tina's doesn't take us too far back in time, because her first, last, and only

Music featured in this episode:

A singalong version of "Closer to Fine," Indigo Girls

"Don't Run Away," King Robbie, featuring Snow

"So Good to See You," Mark Kleiner Power Trio

"Jiggable," Rick Threat

"Doughnut Shop," Paloma

"U.B. the Monster," Metalwood

"Anathemic," Chris Tarry

"Blinded," Dan Gagnon

"Weakness in Me," Joan Armatrading

This Is the Episode in Which . . .

- Alice gets her period, so no-go in the lesbian-impregnator department.

- Alice explains to Jenny what she calls a "hundred-footer": Says Alice,

"It means you can tell she's a lesbian from a hundred feet away. Is it her hair? Is it her jog bra? Is it her mandles? I don't know."

- Jenny comes out to a room full of dykes at the White Party, complete with a dramatic reenactment of the Marina seduction. She exclaims,

"Marina wrecked my fucking life with supposition!" as she re-members Marina telling her, *"I think I'm falling in love with you."*

- Alice registers her disdain for Tonya from the get-go:

"Call me a hippie, but that girl has bad fucking vibes. All right? I mean, and Dana's judgment sucks, right? Except for Lara."

- Tonya tells Dana that she thinks cats are "cold and unfeeling."

girl love is Bette, whom she gets to know at a dinner party she attends with her boyfriend Eric (Kyle Cassie), an entertainment lawyer and art collector. But Shane's tops all: as an eight-year-old she became smitten with Tiffany Gardner (Sarah Widdows) and handed over her Sunshine Meal as an unrequited gesture of love. Even Lenore claims to have a story involving two women making out in a pool—what she won't say is that neither of them was interested in inviting her to join them. When they arrive in Palm Springs, Dana is swept up in Hurricane Tonya, the guest liaison who is determined to hitch her wagon to her charge before the end of the weekend, much to everyone's disgust. And Dana's not the only one leaving Palm Springs with a human souvenir. Jenny makes a date with Robin, a gallant trapeze artist, who saves her from a drink-and-dial call to Marina. At home, Bette invites Candace, a carpenter, to submit a bid to work on the "Provocations" show, and the deal is unexpectedly sealed with a kiss.

L Is for . . . Linking It Up

Title card: Los Angeles, California, 1979

Disco music is blaring at a pool party. People are walking around, dancing, snorting coke. One guy is sitting down, smoking a joint. There are scantily clad waitresses serving drinks. Some men are whooping it up near the pool, cheering on two topless women as they start making out. A third woman gets in the water and they encourage her to join in the fun.

The Link-up

Alice's mother, Lenore Pieszecki, reminisces about this moment from her Hollywood salad days to Alice and her friends on their road trip and, as ever, she embellishes. In her telling, she is the third woman. When we see the scene replayed, however, Lenore is at the end of the pool, looking puzzled and a little scared, and the women—along with everyone else—don't even notice her.

Tonya, played by Meredith McGeachie

Tonya meets Dana when she serves as her guest liaison at the Kraft-Nabisco Professional Women's Golf Tournament. If it isn't love at first sight, she recognizes marriage material when she sees it. But Tonya needs to make a few adjustments: the Ton-Ton is really not a cat person . . . bye-bye, Mr. Piddles. A savvy manager with a gift for PR, Tonya knows just the way to further raise Dana's career profile: turn their wedding into the first corporate-sponsored gay nuptials in history. But the wedding is doomed as soon as their engagement is announced when, unbeknownst to Tonya, Alice plants a kiss on Dana. Ultimately, it is Tonya who calls off the wedding, when Melissa Rivers sweeps Tonya off her feet a few short months later.

Meredith McGeachie received a 2004 Genie Award nomination and a 2002 Vancouver Critics Circle Award for Best Actress in a feature film for the role of Julie in *Punch*. Born in Toowoomba, Australia, and currently splitting her time between Los Angeles, California, and Vancouver, British Columbia, she is a graduate of the George Brown Theatre School in Toronto, Ontario. Coexecutive Producer Rose Troche says, "Meredith was so fucking funny. She's a mensch. She totally took on the role of Tonya and said, 'I will be hated,' and got in there and pulled her pants up!"

Robin, played by Anne Ramsay

Trapeze artist Robin meets Jenny at the White Party during the Dinah Shore weekend, when she rescues her from a drunken, peer-pressured phone call to her torturous ex-lover, Marina. Robin has been betrayed by past lovers and hopes to make up for lost time by getting serious with Jenny. The burden of Robin's expectations scares Jenny more than does the uncertain future, and she breaks it off before the woman gets caught up in the Schecter web of mindfuckery.

Best known for her role as Helen Hunt's sister on *Mad About You,* Anne Ramsay has appeared in many films and on television series, most recently guest-starring on *Monk, Without a Trace,* and the final season of *Six Feet Under.*

"Locked Up": Episode 113

Written by Ilene Chaiken
Directed by Lynne Stopkewich

Clea's infatuation with Shane is wearing down her last nerve. Shane's scare tactics about her drug use and thousands of bedpost notches have instead impressed Clea, a girl who won't take no for an answer. So she tells Clea the truth but keeps it vague: She's in love with "someone." Jenny gets permission from Tim to entertain Robin in her studio-turned-apartment. And that's Friday night. She lines up a Saturday night date when her new literary experiment—a story about a mute woman who can only speak the language of the manatee—sends her to the local aquarium, where she meets a Jewish marine biologist, a guy whom she decides is cute enough to give heterosexuality another go. Everyone at The Planet wants to partner up with Kit. With Francesca cutting the purse strings, Marina begs Kit to get into the business with her. And at an event that Kit organizes at The Planet, emcee Ivan Aycock, a sober trans-man and master drag king performer, is courting her old style, helping to keep the singer straight—it's been over a month since Kit has had a single drink. The rest of the crew ends up in the slammer for participating in the riot that breaks out when the Coalition for Concerned Citizens pull an Operation Rescue–like mission to block the shipment of art from entering the CAC. Candace rallies everyone to form a human shield to protect the deliveryman from the protestors. Alice, Shane, Dana, Candace, and Bette are shoved in a paddywagon alongside some choice right-wingers. Bette and Candace form their own coalition when they are put in a cell together and make each other climax just by talkin' dirty through the bars—it lends "mindfuck" a whole new meaning.

This Is the Episode in Which . . .

- Dana entrusts Mr. Piddles to Tonya's care for the first—and last—time.

- Marina makes a play for Jenny's date, Robin, who isn't charmed by the Anne Carson–seduction approach. She's not "a big reader."

- Jenny tells Robin she lost her virginity when she was thirteen to another kid in the back of a car.

- Cherie blows off Shane.

Music featured in this episode:

"Frances and Her Friends," Frances Faye

"Abiento," Tommy Guerrero

"I Am the Man," Philosopher Kings

"Savoir Faire," Willy Deville

"Havana Disco Nap," Paloma

"Buttergroove," Fundamental

"Borrito," Fundamental

"Come," Kinnie Starr

"Genius," Murmurs

"Reddie 2 Partie 1," Mmo

"Always Crawl," Radiogram

125

L Is for . . . Linking It Up

Title card: Off the coast of Florida, April 1999

Dolphins are swimming around in an aquarium to "Frances and Her Friends" by Frances Faye. The dolphins swim together, some in pairs, others in groups. A few of them start mating. Enter the Beluga whales, who come up to the window to say hi.

The Link-up

Jenny goes to the South Coast Aquarium and as she's watching the dolphins and Beluga whales swimming around, she meets a marine biologist, who offers to help her with her research on her latest story about a mute woman who discovers she can speak the language of the manatees.

Guest Director Lynne Stopkewich on "Locked Up":

"The original concept for the episode was supposed to spoof women-in-prison movies. The original script had all the girls getting arrested at the riot in front of the gallery, and then they all get thrown in the slammer and separated. There's a whole food-fight scene and a shower sequence. Shane, Alice, and Dana break out of prison by crawling through an airshaft only to discover that they're still in the prison. Then there are these crazy guards who strip-search them.

"We looked at all of these old women-in-prison movies, some of which Pam Grier was in. They were kind of hilarious. We totally went to town: It was completely fantasy-driven. I think what ended up happening was, at the end of the day, it was decided that the tone of it was so radically different from anything else they had done before that it just didn't fit in. I found out later that all of this footage was cut out. But a lot of fans found out that there was this other material, so there was talk at one point that they would reinstate the director's cut, including all of those original scenes, on the DVD. It's really over the top and funny. I don't think that ever panned out."

Ivan Aycock, played by Kelly Lynch

A vintage-auto mechanic by day, Drag King performer by night, Ivan is a sober, polyamorous trans-man who befriends Kit and helps her get her life back on track. Their friendship is emotionally intimate and borders on romantic until Kit drops by Ivan's unannounced one morning and catches a glimpse of him as a *her,* and the accoutrements that help make him a man. Ivan is mortally embarrassed but doesn't let that get in the way of his decision to invest in The Planet as Kit's silent partner. Just as they begin to reconnect as friends, however, Kit learns that Ivan has had a girlfriend for the past five years, which he has neglected to mention in all the time they've known each other.

Kelly Lynch has appeared in the films *Joe Somebody, Charlie's Angels,* and *Drugstore Cowboy.*

Jennifer Beals says, "As soon as Kelly Lynch becomes Ivan, I'm so besotted, I can't even tell you. I'm just mesmerized. I become this high school girl with a crush when she becomes Ivan. I can't even talk to her. She looks like some version of Johnny Depp. Once, I went up to her and asked, 'Can I photograph you, so I can have a picture for my locker?' [*Laughs*] I have a bunch of pictures of Kelly as Ivan."

"Limb from Limb": Episode 114

Written by Ilene Chaiken
Directed by Tony Goldwyn

Dana returns from her stint behind bars to find that Mr. Piddles has mysteriously died, and Tonya doesn't know how to console her. Alice is certain that "the Ton-Ton" is the culprit and comes to Dana's rescue by putting together a funeral for the P-man, where everyone pays their respects, including Kit's new arm candy, Ivan. So Alice is understandably blown away when the grief-stricken Dana announces that she and Tonya are engaged to be married—and even more surprised when she makes a late-night visit to see Dana and declares her love by way of lip service, and sees it returned in kind. Tim approaches Jenny about filing for divorce from their nonmarriage. Jenny is a bit distracted, as she's torn between two lovers: Gene, her male Jewish marine bi-

Music featured in this episode:

"Roads," Portishead

"Ooh Ma," Paloma

"Keep Your Head On," Mirror Keep

"Levitate" Transientworld

"Sadness," Transientworld

"Vivian," Edison Woods

"I'm Your Man," Leonard Cohen

"In the Sun," Joseph Arthur

"Blowers Daughter," Damien Rice

L Is for . . . Linking It Up

The openers take a decidedly different tack, beginning with the season finale. With one exception, the vignettes are no longer cryptic. They offer glimpses into the lives of the nine woman and, in several instances, their friends, often revealing something that the others don't know and may never learn.

Title Card: Los Angeles, Three Days Ago

Bette parks her car in a garage. Candace pulls into the garage a moment later in her old El Camino. Candace is just about to get out of her car when Bette opens the car door, and, as if she's in trance, gets into the passenger seat. She is looking straight ahead the entire time, ignoring Candace's sympathetic gaze. Bette instructs her to "take me somewhere." Candace puts the key in the ignition and drives.

The Link-up

In the episode, Bette and Candace go to a hotel and finally consummate the passion that has been building between them since their first meeting. They're so hot for each other, they can barely make it to their room. Bette is fully engaged at the hotel, but she appears guilt-ridden and slightly detached during an impromptu encounter at the CAC. Tina sees the two women flirting at the "Provocations" opening, figures out that they've been having an affair, and locks herself into an explosive and sexual battle with Bette before breaking off their eight-year relationship and turning up on Alice's couch.

This Is the Episode in Which . . .

• Tim hits the roof when he discovers that Jenny is seeing a guy.

• Dana and Tonya begin dressing alike.

• Tonya spots Melissa Rivers at the "Provocations" opening and chases her down to say hello.

• Tina calls the CAC in pursuit of Candace to discuss a job at the Headquarters for Social Justice while the carpenter is nailing Bette in a nearby hotel room.

• Jenny takes Gene to the "Provocations" opening and runs into Tim and Trish, and then Marina and Robin, before heading out.

• Cherie has a brutal encounter with Shane at "Provocations," telling her,

"What if, in the time we spent together, I felt more alive than I have in the last twenty years of my life? What if that were true? Do you think that I would leave my husband, my child, my houses in Bel Air and East Hampton, my trips to Paris, my black-tie galas to run to some rank little love nest with a twenty-five-year-old assistant hairdresser who barely has her foot in the door? In this fucking ugly world, that kind of love does not exist."

ologist, and Robin, the female trapeze artist. The only one feeling like a fool is the spurned Marina, who is behaving like a desperate shrew. The café proprietor, who has been trying to sabotage Jenny's burgeoning relationship with Robin, makes one final play for her heart via a message on her answering machine, begging for one more chance. Clea detonates a bomb when she tells her parents that she and Shane are madly in love, which puts Cherie on the warpath. Shane's attempts at setting things right serve only to trigger the explosion: An envious Clea spies the two women locked in a teary embrace, and Shane has suddenly and devastatingly become the Jaffe family's number one enemy. Tina is putting in more hours at the Headquarters for Social Justice and fewer serving Bette, who in turn feels a bit entitled to, or maybe slightly less guilty about, her impulsive decision to consummate her lust for Candace the carpenter with hot, frenzied sessions at a nearby hotel and even in her office at the CAC. A discreet affectionate gesture exchanged between the two is glimpsed by Tina at the "Provocations" opening, which tips her off to their affair. Bette returns home to a minefield of assaults—physical and emotional—as an enraged Tina lays into her before fleeing to Alice's apartment for sanctuary.

Guest Director Tony Goldwyn on "Limb from Limb"

"This was my favorite episode to direct for a number of reasons. It was a season finale, so you were paying off all these different story lines. There was great diversity of performances. And when Ilene gave me this script, I thought, Wow, there are six sex scenes in this episode. How do you make six sex scenes original and specific? That sex scene between Bette and Tina was such an interesting opportunity because those two have this dynamic in their relationship where Bette had become so dominant and Tina so subservient, and then when Bette tries to dominate Tina by subduing her when Tina's freaking out about her affair, it becomes sexual. And Tina then tries to dominate her, and makes her make love to her in this weird, violent way. I thought, Hmm, I haven't seen that before. Jennifer and Laurel really went for it. They're really courageous actresses.

"I also learned how time constraints can make you be creative. We had this love scene with Jenny and Gene in the aquarium, and we were pressed for time. It was a long sequence, this sex scene in his office where she starts crying and falling apart. That aquarium was such a cool location, but we didn't have time to get a lot of shots, so I said, We're going to do both scenes in one shot each. We came up with a really cool camera move and utilized that aquarium. It was up to Mia and Tygh Runyan to make sure this three-page scene held. We dollied [pushed] into them—that ocean in the background was great—and then we go into his office, and it was all in one shot, with all the turtles and seals swimming behind them, and they start to have sex against the window and she starts to cry and he's like, What, what is it, what'd I do? It was a tall order for them, but it was exciting because it was working. If you did that one hundred times, you'd never get that right. Those kinds of things were exhilarating. The actors did great work."

L Is for Lovefaking

Demystifying the Sex Scene

Lust would seem to be one of the key L words on the show, because there can be as many as six sex scenes in a fifty-minute episode. According to Ilene Chaiken, this is because "sex tells a story unto itself. It's one of the biggest stories of our human lives. Our sexuality, our orientation, our relationship to sex, and the many ways we have sex are huge parts of who we are. But I won't do a sex scene unless it's telling a story. Each sex scene has a different style and method. The sex tells us who the characters are and what they're going through emotionally—it has to be specific." Erin Daniels, Jennifer Beals, and Rachel Shelley shed some light on what it's like to "fake" love with so many beautiful women:

"Leisha and I were making out on the set all the time during the second season, and then we'd go out and have dinner. We would turn to one another and say, 'Yeah, that was a good scene. I felt really good about that.' It's kind of weird, but you get used to it and start to think of it as a job."—Erin Daniels

Love These Searing Sexual Encounters

Here are seven sex scenes that are as memorable for their erotic potency as they are for their emotional intensity.

1. Bette and Tina's reconnection sex, from "The Pilot"

To their friends, Bette and Tina's seven-year relationship appears perfect. But three rounds in the ring with a couples therapist, an ego-crushing sperm-donor search that includes an unexpected clash over the donor's race, and an aborted *ménage à trois* with a guy who won't share his seed with dykes in need are just a few indications that Bette and Tina are struggling to connect. After a potential donor leaves in a huff, Tina guides Bette's hand between her legs and tells her, "This is you," sparking a ravishing, emotionally charged, and sexually voracious lovemaking session that not only reminds them of their powerful attraction to each other but also renews their faith in the relationship.

"All of the love scenes that I've done have been highly, highly choreographed to the point where I remember Laurel Holloman saying she started to feel like Fred Astaire when describing the scene we did at the end of the pilot. In a fight scene, you wouldn't let an actor just punch at somebody. It's dangerous, and if a camera doesn't see what it needs to see, then it's useless. So everything needs to be choreographed: all the fight scenes, all the love scenes."

—Jennifer Beals

2. Tim and Jenny on the couch, from "The Pilot"

There's something for everyone when Jenny and Tim get funky on the couch. Jenny is straddling Tim's lap, tantalizing him with a story about the two women she saw that afternoon "getting way down" in the swimming pool next door. With each detail she shares, Jenny takes off another article of Tim's clothing. And as she waxes on about the blond girl's beautiful breasts and whispers into Tim's ear about the way the dark-haired woman fucks the blond girl in the pool, he can't pace himself anymore, and neither can we. Pants are off . . . and panting is in full swing.

3. Jenny and Marina's first time, from "The Pilot"

Angst-ridden sex can be hot, especially when it involves a predator as sultry as Marina Ferrer. The emotion Jenny tries to mask is raw and pure: her hands cover the tears streaming across her face while Marina goes down on her. Yes, it's true that some people weep when they are writhing in ecstasy, but Jenny is fraught with guilt.

4. Shane and Cherie in Cherie's dressing room, from "Luck, Next Time"

Shane is summoned to Cherie Jaffe's fabulous mansion for a housecall and gets a delicious surprise when the lady of the house takes off her robe and requests some bodywork. The mere sight of Cherie unbuttoning Shane's shirt and begging for action is hot . . . and that's just the prelude. And nothing amps up the excitement quite like the threat of being caught: Cherie's husband nearly walks in on them.

5. Bette and Candace in the jail cell, from "Locked Up"

The carpenter and the museum director generate a lot of heat when they are together, whether Candace is topping Bette in a no-tell hotel or Bette is guiding Candace's hand down her pants behind closed doors at the CAC. But the truest testament to their chemistry is when the two of them are locked together in a jail cell with a guard hovering nearby. Their mere proximity is enough to wind them up, but when Bette tries to create a safe distance by crossing the room, she finds that desire is as confining as, well, a jail cell. Bette leaves Candace on the cot and walks over to the wall and, with her back to her cellmate, tells her that she is fucking her. They both shudder as they fantasize themselves into a froth, and after imagining it for ourselves, we're not far behind.

6. Alice and Dana's first sex-capade, from "Labyrinth"

Kudos to the music supervisor for cuing up Ce Ce Peniston's "Finally"—finally, indeed! It was inevitable that the comic heart and soul of the show would eventually consummate the love that they declared to each other at the end of the first season. So what if the timing wasn't especially mindful—these two friends jump each other while stuffing naughty little gift bags for Dana and Tonya's upcoming engagement party. Lust knows no bounds. When Dana and Alice get together, *The L Word*'s most whimsical and endearing sex scene ensues, which includes their own brand of slapstick involving couture and a hilarious send-up of *9 1/2 Weeks*.

7. Tina and Helena in the pool at the Chateau Marmont, from "Lagrimas del Oro"

As gorgeous as Helena is, she is off-puttingly haughty. And Tina is hugely pregnant, but she manages to bring out Helena's tender side. When you plunk these two stunners together in a fancy pool, their chemistry is electrifying. And lesbian sex with a pregnant woman marked a first in television history.

"The scene in the Chateau Marmont pool with Laurel was a difficult shot for me to do because it was my first full-on lesbian scene that I was shooting, and it was with a pregnant woman with very large breasts, and, well, that was quite a shock, really [*laughs*]. But because Laurel and I had been working together at that point for a few weeks, and getting along very well, she made me feel very comfortable and very welcome. Director Jeremy Podeswa choreographed all of the action. On camera, it is a bit of a shock. I can remember Jeremy, after the first take, saying 'We need just a bit more . . .'"

—Rachel Shelley

L Is for Looks
The L Wardrobe

Since the show's premiere, the women of *The L Word* have been exploding myths left and right, making us forget every bad lesbian joke in the book (Birkenstocks, vests, and fannypacks, anyone?), thanks to the award-winning costume designer Cynthia Summers, key hair stylist Paul Edwards, and key makeup stylist JoAnn Fowler. Cynthia gives readers an exclusive look inside the L Wardrobe, JoAnn and Paul lend a few beauty secrets, and cast member Leisha Hailey weighs in, keeping *The L Word*'s lesbian street cred in check.

Determining *The L Word* Aesthetic

Cynthia Summers, Costume Designer: During the first season, we were testing the waters with all of the characters. We weren't sure exactly what *The L Word* was going to be and how it was going to be received. We knew who the target audience was, but of course Showtime wanted a broader audience than just the lesbian community of Los Angeles. We wanted to push the envelope, but how far could we go, looks-wise? We didn't want to put everyone off right from the get-go, and we didn't want to be written off as just another *Sex and the City* with pretty girls wearing pretty clothes and having fabulous hair and doing unrealistic things. And this is the first time we've had a show for the girls. With it comes a lot of responsibility.

"We have our staples—everyone wears Prada clothes, shoes, and sunglasses."

Dramatic Dress-up

Cynthia Summers: For every wardrobe fitting, we have to think about what's going to happen in the episode in each scene for each character. I think, Okay, this character is reacting to this and going there in the future, so she wants to be really careful about what she's wearing in this specific instance because it's gonna speak volumes about what she's saying. Oh, and she's got two seconds on film to show it. On TV, you don't have a lot of screen time to show those transitions.

Shopping for the L Wardrobe

Cynthia Summers: We have so many designers we use on the show. We have our staples—everyone wears Prada clothes, shoes, and sunglasses—and then we have a lot of smaller indigenous designers in LA as well, which is great. That's something we're trying to do on the

show . . . trying to keep it in LA. Keep it real, yeah! We get such fantastic pieces of clothing in here that [when it arrives, the actresses] all rush in. Five of them are around the same size, and some of the pieces can go from one to the other. I shop in LA about every two to three weeks. They'll ask, When are you coming back? And they'll be here first thing that morning. Did she come in, did she come in? They're like little kids [*laughs*]. I like to shop locally in LA at boutiques. On Sunset, I love Electric Barbarella, The Way We Wore, and Elmer Ave. for skater/rocker-wear. I really like Yunni at Fred Segal Santa Monica. There are these lesbian designers called Family Evolutions, who have been really generous and supportive of the show. The cast's favorite vintage shop is True Value Vintage.

Designs on the Cast: Hot Couture

Cynthia Summers: There are designers who send things to us. Gianfranco Ferré is one of the designers who came forward and sends me stuff. The dresses in the opening credits are almost exclusively Ferré. They love the show, and they love Jennifer. So does BCBG Max Azria—they've loved Jennifer for a long time, even before the show. Ferré has got a real sculpted edge to his evening wear. Bette wore a Ferré dress to the Peabody Awards dinner that was honoring Tina. Her dress was so amazing. It was very fitted below the knee—Jennifer will only wear things below the knee—and it had a built-in, very high collar with a built-in tie and a very low V-neck. It had a little bit of an S&M vibe to it, and a bit of a man's edge, but it was very tastefully done. You put a woman's body in it, and it's like, Wow! You want to know who this woman is. I think that's the thing about dressing lesbians. Well, you don't have to be a lesbian, of course, to pull this off, but maybe that's why these women are willing to go with this wardrobe and put that kind of edge on it—they want to really wear it like a man. And they're wearing it partly like a man but for other women.

The Inevitability of Hair Extensions

Paul Edwards, Key Hair Stylist: Every one of our main characters has to wear hair extensions—well, except one: Rachel Shelley, who has the most beautiful hair. You never want to add one strand of hair to hers. Seriously, everybody has extensions at some point, and not because they lack hair. Extensions let you change things up so much. If we have a flashback five years earlier, you can throw in some highlights that aren't coloring their real hair—you're just throwing in extensions of a different color. So then you still have the identity of that character, but it takes you to a different time in their life, so people look at it and know it. We also have to add hair extensions at times to people who are getting haircuts by Shane.

"Every one of our main characters has to wear hair extensions."

On the Cast's Natur-L Beauty

JoAnn Fowler, Key Makeup Stylist: We don't do a lot of body makeup—most of the girls are pretty free about being seen as they are. The women are all so beautiful, and all so different, too. It's a joy to actually come in to work. They're all very easy and pretty secure with their characters. We meet with Ilene and the director of the episode, and discuss anything in particular that needs to be addressed. We get the script about three days before a shoot. Any big makeup and hair things we usually try to put at the end of the schedule. One exception was with Kelly Lynch, who was cast as Ivan a day and a half before. We were given the image of Willy DeVille and we ran with it. That was our quickest turnaround ever. For the most part, though, we really just work with the actors, and style her according to her character.

"I purchase British men's shirts for Bette, with bigger collars and longer sleeves, and get great custom cuff links."

Cynthia on dressing Jennifer: "She's got her work look and her going-out look. She doesn't really have a casual look. She's all power suits, out there in the workforce, as the curator of a gallery, so she has to have a bit of an artistic edge to what she wears. We dress her in a lot of Stella McCartney, Dolce & Gabbana, BCBG Max Azria, Gucci, YSL, Valentino, Roland Mouret, and Gianfranco Ferré suits, and from LA, Sheri Bodell and Louis Verdad. Jennifer comes with a big following and large designer fan base, so it's been easy to dress her in beautiful clothes, and she wears them so well. It makes a lot of sense for Bette to wear fabulous clothes—if any character on the show can afford it, it's Bette. I purchase British men's dress shirts for her, with bigger collars and longer sleeves, and get great custom cuff links and then take them in so they are more fitted. They give a nice contrast to the women's suits that she's wearing. It lends them a tougher edge. We get a lot of really great compliments from a lot of professional lesbians about the way Jennifer dresses. When I go to Fashion Week the questions always begin with Jennifer and her wardrobe—always."

JoAnn on making up Jennifer: "Since she's very high powered, we keep her makeup simple and very classic."

Cynthia Summers on dressing Katherine: "Her look has evolved with her character. When we first met her, she was basically just off the street, more or less living out of her car. Her back story is that she was a street kid who turned to sex for money, so she was wearing a bit of leather and had more of a gay male aesthetic. I'm not exactly sure how she got in with this crowd of women, but she started to evolve into a more mature person and developed her hairdressing career. She starts to really find herself in the second season. She's established herself as a well-known hairdresser, so her look cleaned up as far as that grungy street and leather thing goes, and her partying has calmed down a little. We fashioned her a little bit the first season from the street to late '60s Mick Jagger mixed in with a bit of Keith Richards, plus her hair and everything was a little bit of Warren Beatty from *Shampoo*. She wears Levi's, Converse, J. Lindeberg, Viktor & Rolf, and local skate/rocker designer Jonny Day at Elmer Ave.—tons of vintage and homespun clothes."

JoAnn on making up Katherine: "Her character started out hiding and very boyish. As we've gone along, and we've gotten to know her, she's gotten a lighter look. As her character gets emotionally healthier, she looks healthier. We have a fairly good idea at the beginning of the season where the character is going to end up, so we can judge how we can adjust things."

Cynthia on dressing Pam: "I'm so happy to be working with Pam. I worked with her once before. I was really nervous the first time I met her, and I'm not very often starstruck, but she is gracious and an icon and a big beautiful woman. On camera and behind the camera she's just like this force to be reckoned with, and if she puts her trust in you, she just puts her trust in you one hundred percent. I could put anything on her and she'd be happy with it. She's not the easiest person to dress on the show for a lot of reasons: Her character is straight and a recovering alcoholic. She's older, much more mature, and she's on a journey as well. And she's a big woman with a figure to die for—she's got all the right curves and solid as a rock, everywhere. But when I put her beside all of the other girls, who are all very tiny twigs, it's tough, and it's very rare that we don't have an episode where they're not standing all together at least once. I never have to use a foundation garment on her. A lot of times we accentuate that killer hourglass figure of hers. She wears Escada, who loves Pam and back. We have her in Etro and St. John for gowns, and local designer Hippy Girl for her ethnic retro look."

Cynthia on dressing Mia: "Jenny is one of the harder characters to dress because you couldn't say, Here this is this character's type. She is having an identity crisis—she is not on a straight and narrow path. Her journey was really unmatched, especially in the first season, so dressing her was a bit of a guessing game. We were following Ilene Chaiken's lead, and Mia's lead, and the story's lead.

"On camera and behind the camera [Pam's] just like this force to be reckoned with, and if she puts her trust in you, she just puts her trust in you one hundred percent. "

Whereas usually we have character arcs that span over a few episodes, and take on a look or a story line for a few episodes, Jenny's character changes moment by moment in every single episode. She's always had a little flapper in her, like when she goes to Burr Connor's house in the second season. Even in her grungier period, and her dark street vintage look, you can see that 1920s look in there: It's in her face, which is classic, with her pale skin and her dark hair. Jenny hides a lot because she's so insecure and has no idea what she's doing most of the time, but then she gets a burst of confidence from I don't know where. Another challenge is keeping hats off of Mia's head because she loves to wear them, and on TV you can't because it's really hard to see people's faces. Her look definitely mirrors exactly where her character is at the moment, and as we all know, it's sort of a scary, bumpy ride. I think that is really reflected in her wardrobe a lot. We dress her in Rebecca Taylor, Magda Berliner in LA, Lanvin, and tons of vintage clothes from Catwalk & Lili et cie, and True Value Vintage. We're really careful not to have her wear labels because Jenny couldn't afford it—I would never put like a Chanel logo on her. When she does wear higher-end clothes, we try to make sure that they mix in with her thrift-store look. A discerning eye might be able to pick out the Dolce & Gabbana and wonder how her character could afford it, and that's true, but, hey, it *is* TV."

Cynthia on dressing Sarah: "The second season was a whole year where we were trying to discover, who is Carmen? We know she is a DJ, a Latina, and the first woman to knock Shane off of her feet since Cherie Jaffe. But we struggled with what kind of lesbian Carmen was and tried to fit Sarah Shahi into that. I'm not so sure we hit our mark in season two, but I know we did in season three. In season two, I saw her feeling her club vibe and trying to work around that shaggy, mullet hair. She dressed like a DJ, with lots of band T-shirts, cut-up or rolled jeans or cargos, sneaks, tattoos, and Organics jewelry. Maybe the problem with this wardrobe for Sarah was it just wasn't different enough from a lot of the other characters, especially in the club scenes—Carmen didn't stand out enough from the crowd. I think the hair change in the third season made a difference. Sarah is just so girly she can't help it. She is so curvy and gorgeous, and in some way we were working against that in the second season, but now "jaw dropping" is the only way to put it. We steered away from her grungy look in the third season, and went more hip-hop and it worked! A little more Latina, more shorts and boots, sexy overalls with just a bikini top underneath. Some sexy skater pieces with embroidered jeans, less jewels. We put her in Dior, anything from Fred Segal, Elmer Ave., Afroman. She also wears a lot of fabulous things from local LA designers like Meghan, Deborah Lindquist. We actually get to see her in a dress a few times in season three. Basically, we needed to show off her killer figure which we totally do! I'm definitely happier with her look and I know Sarah is, too."

JoAnn on making up Sarah: "She doesn't have a real tattoo. Carmen's tattoo is a peel-off. We had that made. It originally came from an idea Ilene had, and we tried to interpret it. Cheryl, the art director, came up with the final piece and I went down to LA and had it made. We get a lot of comments about it, people wondering where she got it."

Cynthia on dressing Laurel: "We buy her a lot of Dolce & Gabbana, and in LA, we find a lot of stuff for her at Fred Segal and Theodore boutiques, who carry a lot of LA designers. We found a lot of her maternity clothes at Marni, Pea in the Pod, and Nom and Lululemon."

JoAnn on making up Laurel: "As with Jennifer, we give Laurel the classic treatment, though her character, Tina, is getting increasingly more glammed up in the third season that she's returning to the office."

Cynthia on dressing Leisha: "I love Leisha. Alice is the roving reporter, which we really played up in season two. When she goes out on jobs, she dresses the part. And when she goes to Dana's country club to see her parents, she dresses in a beautiful little pink blouse and a little skirt, and she put on pearls and she'd carry a purse and even pearl earrings and stuff like that because she wanted to show up for Dana. She wore a lot of Marc Jacobs in second season—head to toe. She also wears Chloe, Twelfth Street by Cynthia Rowley, anything from Barneys New York, and Great China Wall jeans."

"I love Leisha. Alice is the roving reporter, which we really played up in season two."

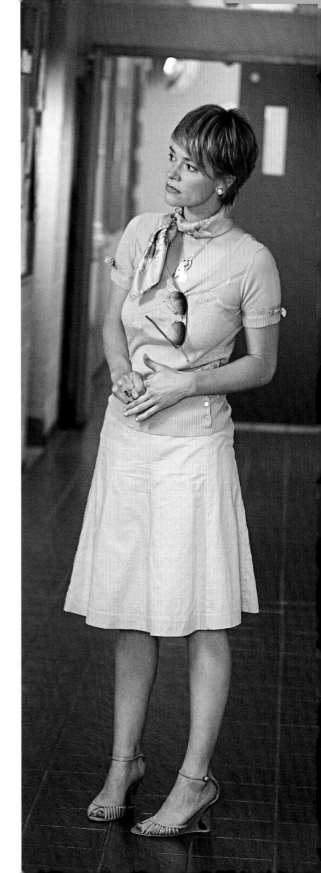

Cynthia on dressing Erin: "She's a jock, so she wears a lot of Adidas and Fila for tennis. But she's also become more style conscious. She wears a lot of Marni, as well as Twelfth Street by Cynthia Rowley, Stella McCartney, Dolce & Gabbana, Lacoste, Prada, and vintage clothes from The Way We Wore."

JoAnn on making up Erin: "Since Dana is an athlete, she's not usually too glamorous, so we go more natural unless she's going out to a party."

Cynthia on dressing Rachel: "Helena is an English style maven and has money to spare. She wears Proenza Schouler, Stella McCartney, YSL, Prada, Ann Demeulemeester, Valentino, and Jenny Packham London."

JoAnn on making up Rachel: "Because Helena is so rich, her character is always done."

"Helena is an English style maven and has money to spare."

Strappy Trappings: Accessorizing from Head to Toe

Cynthia on jewelry: "As with anything else, the jewelry must be reflective of the character. Bette's jewels range mostly from artistically inspired pieces to traditionally inspired pieces, as befits her personality and environment: She is a professional in the art world. On a personal level, Jennifer rarely goes before camera without earrings, a necklace, and a watch. Maybe it's a comfort thing, or maybe that is her way of feeling complete in her look—the final touches! On TV, most shots are what's called the "cowboy" shot, which is when the camera hits you above the waist or chest, so we really concentrate on the details around the upper body. It's a bummer, because we have a killer shoe collection on this show, and every single one of the girls has a shoe fetish! Lots of times when building a look, I'll start with the shoes if I'm stumped for something fresh. Shoes and jewelry, I think, most reflect who we really are, for good and bad!

"I shop for several different options of jewelry for each outfit. Most of the jewelry comes from Blue Ruby in Vancouver, but we also get great stuff from Chan Luu in LA, David Yurman in New York, and Karen Astrachan in Connecticut. Then we have the fitting, determine the outfit, and embellish it with jewels, hats, bags, et cetera. A lot of times, if we love a piece but may

"There is nothing worse than holding up camera with dozens of people on set because of a fashion crisis: Someone doesn't want to wear this piece of jewelry today or her shoes hurt or this one's jeans are too tight."

not use it with this particular change, we'll keep it for down the road. Also, a few of our cast members like to have an option on the day of shooting, just in case. There is nothing worse than holding up camera with dozens of people on set because of a fashion crisis: Someone doesn't want to wear this piece of jewelry today or her shoes hurt or this one's jeans are too tight. You always have options. We fortunately have huge amounts of jewelers who loan pieces to the show. I am always on the lookout for quiet jewelers, the ones who value their pieces as art and don't commercially promote them.

"Pam is a woman who loves embellishing stuff and, boy, does she love color. During the first season, sometimes I let the women choose their own jewelry and accessories if the outfit is really lacking in color or something. I'd just put a bunch of jewelry out, and three girls would be in the room, and I'd say, Pick a necklace out or some earrings—it doesn't really matter to me. I'm happy with what you pick. So, the first few times I go into Pam's trailer. She would have almost everything on her body, and say, What do you think? And then Pam was serious. I'd say, Okay, maybe not that. And then we'd start to undress her. Bless her heart—Pam does everything two hundred percent—I love her to death."

Cynthia on the "sole" of *The L Word:* "If Manolo Blahnik was the shoe for *Sex and the City,* Christian Louboutin is the official shoe for *The L Word.* We love those shoes on the show, especially Mia. Jennifer is a Gucci girl. We get a lot of different shoes for her, but shoes ground her. She feels good in one pair and she'll probably wear that pair out until I can get another pair on her feet. Which is not to say that she doesn't like shoes. But for a lot of suit looks we always fall back to that favorite pair of Gucci stiletto pumps that go with everything. Pam loves Stuart Weitzman boots, and Leisha is Balenciaga boots all the way. We have not a single pair of Birkenstocks on the set, so far. These girls opt for Uggs, which are a bit more indicative of Los Angeles—those appear to be the only comfort shoe on camera."

[Side note: The author spied the elegant Londoner Rachel Shelley sporting a pair of Birkenstocks in the privacy of her own trailer. Could Birks become the new Uggs in a couple of years? After all, London is one of the trendsetting capitals of the Western world.]

Baggage Claim

Cynthia on lesbians and purses: "We have a surplus of Fendi, Hermès, Trina Turk, but one thing I had to battle at the very beginning was the notion that lesbians don't wear dresses or carry purses. Because Leisha is out, she was the one that I looked to for real hardcore authority. And I dressed everyone from head to toe: shoes, bags, jewelry. Usually when I do a fitting, I present everything, and then we pull back from there. I remember one of my first fittings with Leisha: She was preparing to go out. And, it must be said that of all our girlie-girls, Leisha is the most likely to wear a dress. She is the girliest—a clotheshorse, she will dress up for an occasion. So Leisha is wearing a vintage A-line dress. I had the purse for her. Leisha's so gracious and polite. She's like, 'Oh, really?' And I said, 'Yeah, yeah, this looks great! It's not too feminine, but you'll need something. You're going to this dinner.' And she tells me, 'Cynthia, lesbians don't carry purses.' And I said, 'Well, I think you really need one in this scene. It really works well in this scene, and why not? Push the envelope.' So she's going along with it. A couple of weeks later, she returns from visiting her girlfriend after her birthday and she's got a new Louis Vuitton bag—it was white with the multicolored LVs all over it, and pink bows. She says, 'Look what I've got! Nina bought it for me.' And I said, 'Leisha! Wow! But I thought lesbians didn't carry purses.' And she said, 'Yeah, I know. But I love it.'"

Leisha Hailey explains: "At first I was telling Cynthia, I don't think dykes dress like this. And, yes, my big thing at the beginning was that dykes don't wear purses. This lesbian comedienne Suzanne Westenhoefer has this joke about how awful it is if you're the one dyke who carries the purse, because you'll go out and everybody'll be like, Hey, can I put my keys in there? But I went through a purse phase. I'm out of it now. But at the time, I thought, This is great! You just put everything in this little bag and you go! [*Laughs.*] I'm so used to my keys and my wallet and always packing them in my pants. But since the show debuted, when I go into gay bars in LA, I do see a difference in what women are wearing. And some are even wearing purses."

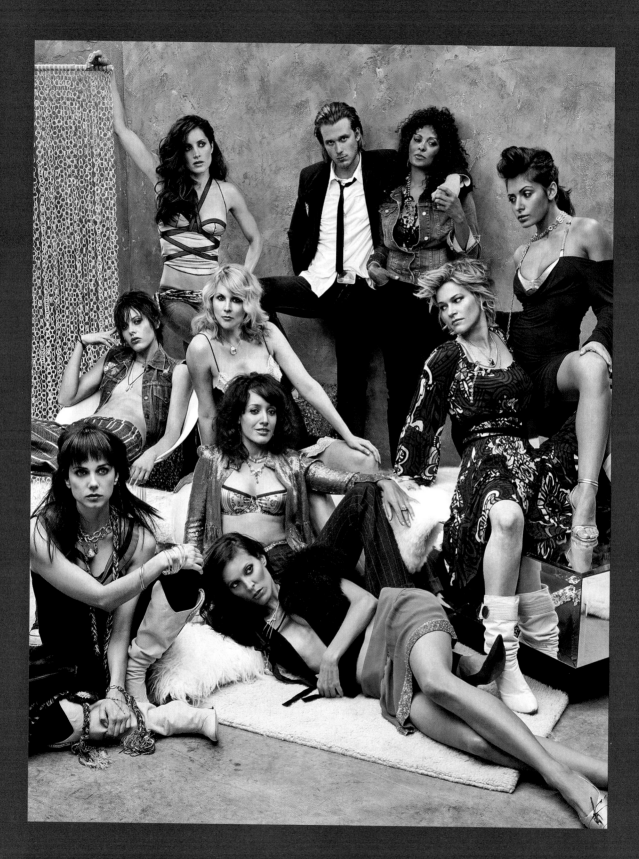

Season TWO
Episode Guide

The *L Word* has had a makeover since the first season, both in its overall presentation and the women themselves. Gone is the enigmatic synthesizer-blip music that accompanied a rainstorm of L words across the screen, and in comes an original theme song by BETTY called "The Way That We Live" that manages to be at once in your face and melodious, paired with a flashy and feverish music-video montage of our favorite gals portrayed as unabashed LA fashion plates, decked out in couture by Gianfranco Ferré.

But underneath the fabulous clothes are the women about whom we've come to care deeply. Tina has moved out of the home she shared with Bette, couch hopping before settling into her own apartment. Though the timing couldn't be worse, she is finally pregnant, and she has no qualms about raising the baby on her own if it means recovering her autonomy, which had all but disappeared in her relationship with Bette. Work has always defined Bette, or so she believes, but her struggle to maintain her position at the CAC intensifies by the day. And when her father, Melvin, is diagnosed with terminal cancer, she realizes that without Tina, she feels totally unmoored. Overwhelmed with regret for her affair, Bette fights to recover their relationship, and coparent their child. But Peggy Peabody's scheming daughter, Helena (new cast member Rachel Shelley), arrives from New York and threatens to sabotage every area of Bette's life. Shane is left numb after being frozen out by Cherie Jaffe, and she is determined to stay that way. Then she meets the diehard romantic Carmen de la Pica Morales (new cast member Sarah Shahi)—a production assistant-cum-DJ, who falls in love with her at first sight and becomes determined to thaw her out. Marina has returned to Italy, and Tim has moved to Ohio, leaving a penniless Jenny with the house but no strong connection to anyone in West Hollywood. So when she invites Shane to move in, she not only eases her financial problems but gains a new best friend—a necessary source of support for the painful soul-searching journey on which she is about to embark. The alliance is especially crucial when their third roommate, videographer Mark Wayland (new cast member Eric Lively), peers too closely into their lives, conjuring up the memory of a devastating trauma Jenny has suppressed for years. Alice and Dana are forced to reckon with their mutual attraction. Consummation comes with serious consequences. Are they willing to risk everything, including, quite possibly, their friendship? With her bad business track record and ambitious plans, Kit would seem ill-advised to take over The Planet. But she's never been more together, and her forecast vastly improves when she meets a man who teaches her how to keep her business in the black. If only their tortured romance could keep her heart from ever broaching the blues.

"Life, Loss, Leaving": Episode 201
Written by Ilene Chaiken
Directed by Dan Minahan

I n the time Tina has spent on Alice's couch since breaking up with Bette, her abdomen has grown considerably larger. Her friends think she's eating her pain. But unbeknownst to everybody, especially Bette, who hasn't called Tina since their huge fight over a month ago, she's actually eating for two. Jenny is still negotiating her three-ring circus, juggling a female trapeze artist, a male marine biologist, and the looming presence of her angry ex-fiancé. The men are the first to skip out: An exasperated, undersexed Gene sets Jenny straight by telling her she's "a girl-loving full-on lesbian." And Tim takes a coaching job at Oberlin in Ohio, leaving her with the lease and a month of free rent—a mixed blessing for Jenny, who is waitressing at a

This Is the Episode in Which . . .

- Tonya exclaims, "Bette is still shtupping the carpenter?"

- Tina flips a table at The Planet at Bette, accidentally hurling hot creamy beverages all over Tonya, yelling, "Did you fuck all night before you told [Candace] I was the love of your life this morning?!"

- Alice hosts a knitting circle in her apartment. A woman looks at the pink tube-shaped collar she's been knitting and says, "Dear, I don't think you're gonna be able to get anybody's head through that thing." Alice examines it, nods, and responds, "You know, though, I think this would make a really good harness for a strap-on dildo."

- Alice makes her alliance to Tina known to Bette for the first time.

Bette: *"You know, Tina abandoned me as much as I abandoned her. We both did it."*

Alice: *"Yeah, but only one of you was having an orgasm."*

trendy, cheap diner, has few friends, and recoils at the thought of Robin with a U-Haul. If Jenny interprets Tim's act of generosity as one of forgiveness, he sets her straight with a drunken, rage-fueled sexual encounter before taking off for the Midwest. Marina has a parting gift, too, and Jenny is the last to hear about it. Everyone at The Planet is talking about her alleged suicide attempt, but no one can agree on her method. Only one thing is certain: Her absence is very present, and the café will never be the same . . . for better or for worse. Now that Alice and Dana have acknowledged their mutual attraction, they resolve to make another of their impossible pacts, promising to steer clear of seductive venues when they are together—bathrooms, cars, their respective apartments, places with tables . . . or floors. Dana doesn't want to break her engagement to Tonya, but resisting Alice is getting increasingly difficult. After being burned by Cherie Jaffe, Shane is willing herself to avoid love at all costs, even when it appears in its foxiest form: production assistant/DJ Carmen de la Pica Morales, a headstrong romantic she meets at a hair gig for Arianna Huffington (who guest stars as herself). Carmen can't even pretend to be casual about sex. Kit is getting her life together—she's meeting with Marina's family to buy The Planet and has gotten her driver's license back—so auto mechanic Ivan presents her with two gifts to celebrate the occasion. He's pimped Kit's ride, and he gives her a key to his place. When Kit drops by unannounced one day, she catches a glimpse of Ivan's dildo in its harness resting on his dresser, and of Ivan himself as "she" emerges from the bathroom. Ivan is so humiliated that he banishes her from the apartment and retreats from their increasingly intimate friendship. Bette awakens in bed with Candace and realizes she wants out, but Tina is far from ready to let her back into her heart.

Music featured in this episode:

"Just a Little Lovin'," Dusty Springfield

"Next Flight," Transientworld

"Nighttime in the Desert," Rainwater Bluegrass Band

"Devil's Daughter," Rainwater Bluegrass Band

"Temptress," Fundamental

"Honey's in Love," Flunk

"Threes and Fours," Mike Clarke

"Nearer," Kinnie Starr

"Sweet Angel," Donnie Owens

"History," Controller, Controller

"Serious Trouble," Zongamin

"Lonely, Lonely," Feist

L Is for . . . Linking It Up

Title Card: Los Angeles, Present Day

These are two vignettes that jump-cut back and forth between Tina and Bette. Tina is at the office of her ob-gyn, Dr. Wilson, discussing her past miscarriage and how it has affected her future decision about when she would have disclosed the fact of her pregnancy to Bette . . . if they were still together. She turns to face Dr. Wilson, and we see that Tina has a very swollen, pregnant belly. She explains to Dr. Wilson that for now, she is going to keep her pregnancy to herself. She plans on raising the baby alone.

As Tina lays this out for Dr. Wilson, we are flashed glimpses of Bette and Candace making love.

The Link-up

The scene following the credits shows Bette and Candace in bed. Initially, Bette is smiling, but she disengages and a look of concern and panic washes over her face.

At The Planet, Alice is recounting the breakup story for Shane, Dana, and Tonya. We learn that Bette hasn't called Tina since their breakup a month earlier. This is soon remedied by an upsetting encounter between the exes when Bette approaches Tina at the café with a teary apology, news that she's broken it off with Candace, and a plea for forgiveness. The whole spectacle infuriates Tina.

Tina's rage sets the drama in motion for the season: Bette discovers how lost she is without Tina, and conversely, Tina realizes her self-sufficiency and regains a sense of autonomy. And, true to her word in Dr. Wilson's office, Tina doesn't tell anyone about her pregnancy until the third episode. She first informs Alice. Bette is the last to know—she finds out in "Labyrinth."

Arianna Huffington, playing herself

Shane is hired to do the hair of political pundit Arianna Huffington to prepare her for a television appearance. As she finishes styling her, a sexy production assistant named Carmen de la Pica Morales brings coffee for the commentator. Arianna is fascinated as she watches the two women flirt and decides to cut Shane loose so that she can pursue Carmen.

Arianna Huffington is an activist, syndicated columnist, and journalist, and has written biographies of Maria Callas and Pablo Picasso.

"Lap Dance": Episode 202

Written by Ilene Chaiken
Directed by Lynne Stopkewich

The Planet is temporarily closed and the girls feel displaced and strangely beholden to Tonya, who is able to translate the coffee menu from the franchise café across the street. Kit appreciates that Ivan was mortified by their last encounter, but with the imminent arrival of Marina's family, she has no choice but to crash his remote cabin and beg him to consider investing in The Planet. Ivan comes in at the last minute as a silent partner, which enables her to close the deal. Kit and Bette are in for a huge surprise when they meet Count Manfredi Ferrer (Derek de Lint), who they presume to be Marina's father. But Manfredi is quick to correct them: He has been married to Marina for twelve years! Tonya endears herself to Sharon and Irwin Fairbanks—helping Dana to make strides in gaining a new level of acceptance from them—when she shares a heartrending story about her former fiancé's proposal to "not marry" her. Shane rebukes Alice for recommending that Tina consult Joyce Wischnia (Jane Lynch), a leading gay civil rights lawyer, to explore the possibility of seeking a separa-

This Is the Episode in Which . . .

• The Organ performs in the first of a series of live musical performances this season.

• We see cigar-chomping feminist lawyer Joyce Wischnia hurling Velcro balls onto a big felt uterus wall hanging—her favorite office toy.

• Joyce tells Tina: "In the eyes of the world, especially the world as embodied by the courts, you are shit. You gave up your autonomy in a relationship that the law doesn't recognize. And your ex controls everything."

• Dana shows her friends that she has totally succumbed to lesbian codependence when she allows Tonya to speak for her at the café: "She likes what I like. She always wants what I want more than what she wants. Right?"

• Writing teacher Charlotte Birch knocks Jenny down a few notches when she says of "Thus Spoke Sarah Schuster":

"Arrogant is fine. Hubristic, overly precious bad puns are to be avoided, especially if she wants to get into my class."

• Shane asks Alice if she and Dana are "getting it on yet" and assures her that no one else is onto them.

Music featured in this episode:

"Why?" Fundamental

"Brother," performed live by The Organ

"Un Homme et Une Femme," Coco Love Alcorn

"Formatt Flute," Fundamental

"From Foreign Lands," Schumann

"Limboland," BETTY

"Hop Up Ladies," Dan Zanes

"Endless," Silk Road Music

"Heathcha," Hipjoint

"She's Mine," Hipjoint

"Ilya," Martina Topley-Bird

"How to Be a Lady," Erin McKeown

Charlotte Birch, played by Sandra Bernhard

A fiction writer teaching an exclusive workshop at CU, Charlotte Birch chafes at work that draws on obvious autobiographical information. She is a shrewd critic with a sharp tongue and refuses to indulge her students, especially Jenny. But she eventually warms to her, and even gets Jenny a ghostwriting gig with closet-case Hollywood action star Burr Connor.

Sandra Bernhard is one of American's most unsparing observers and daring comedic performers. She regularly appears on talk shows and guest stars on a variety of television programs, but she's perhaps best known for her one-woman shows, *I'm Still Here . . . Damn It!* and *Without You, I'm Nothing,* as well as her brilliant film debut in Martin Scorsese's *The King of Comedy.*

tion agreement from Bette. Shane suggests Tina instead get a lap dance. Tina scores by getting both. Carmen gets a bit of lip service from Shane—snogs and an explanation of her no-strings-attached policy. Jenny desperately wants to get into a master class at CU with writer Charlotte Birch—who is not taking an instant shine to "Sarah Schuster"—and out of a fledgling relationship with Robin, whose intentions become clear when she introduces her to friends, eager to know about their plans to start a family. Bette has never felt more alone now that Tina is consulting a lawyer, and the rest of their circle have turned against her; all of them, that is, except for Shane, a true diplomat and loyal friend, and Jenny, who knows what it is like to be vilified for an indiscretion. An impromptu front-porch hangout with Bette one evening inspires Jenny to invite Shane to be her new roommate.

L Is for . . . Linking It Up

Title Card: Mendocino, California, 2003

Robin walks out of a church wearing a white tuxedo. People are throwing rice, and she's looks happy until she gets to the bottom of the steps and realizes her new spouse, Claybourne, is nowhere to be found. Cut to a room inside the church where we see Claybourne making out with a beautiful woman.

The Link-up

Robin takes Jenny to meet her friends, who are older and coupled. The friends interrogate Robin and especially Jenny about their future plans to marry and have children, and then they enumerate all the unhealthy aspects of Robin's previous relationship with the caddish Claybourne, who cheated on her on their wedding day. Jenny feels overwhelmed by the pressure from Robin and her friends and decides to break things off.

Guest Director Lynne Stopkewich says:

"We shot the lap dance scene in a really well-known Vancouver strip club—not a lesbian bar. It was pretty funny. There are so many women on the production crew and on the cast. We went in there, and I immediately jumped up on the stage and grabbed the brass pole. We all started laughing because all of the women started jumping up on the stage. We were like, Wow! So this is what it would feel like to be up here? That happens a lot on the show, this reappropriation of things that have been on the other side, objectification and representation, so that's always great to have an opportunity to reclaim it."

"Loneliest Number": Episode 203
Written by Lara Spotts
Directed by Rose Troche

Tina test drives her new lawyer by letting Joyce call a meeting with Bette and her lawyer to discuss their potential separation. Bette tries to appeal directly to Tina, who stonewalls her, revealing her new-and-improved unyielding side. Tina accepts Joyce's invitation to move off of Alice's couch and into her guesthouse. Kit tells Shane and Alice of her plans to turn The Planet into a music venue by night, but gets nervous when she realizes that the R&B musical acts she's lined up for opening night don't jibe with the girls. Alice promises Kit that she will help her maintain her Sapphic clientele through the power of the lesbian phone tree by hooking her up with Pink. Failing that—and she does fail at pinning down the pop superstar—she delivers on BETTY (Elizabeth Ziff, Amy Ziff, Alyson Palmer,

Music featured in this episode:

"Jungle Jane," BETTY

"I Never Knew Your Name," Joystick

"Andante," Schubert

"Menuetto Allegretto," Schubert

"Hold Me Now," Thompson Twins

"Good Good Good," Joystick

"Anything," Kinnie Starr

"Basement Band Song," The Organ

"Steven Smith," The Organ

"Pinch the Box," Stinkmitt

"Super Bad Girl," Iffy

"Love Strikes Hard," Carole Pope

"Light Bright City," Transientworld

"Bangin on My Clit," Stinkmitt

"It Girl," BETTY

"Some Kind of Wonderful," performed live by Pam Grier and BETTY

This Is the Episode in Which . . .

• Tina sits out the reopening party of The Planet to apply for a Peabody Grant for the Headquarters for Social Justice, which puts her in direct competition with Bette.

• Alice tells Tina, "Remember how I used to tell you it would suck if you and Bette broke up? Well, it does. This is so fucked. You know, I'm starting to get scared. It's like, Bette's smoking and drinking herself to death and you're—I'm gonna say it, Tina—you're eating your pain! And I don't know how much weight you've gained, but if you don't stop, you're gonna have to go to some ashram, or hire some really majorly important trainer and you don't have the money!"

• As Bette and Jenny bond over losing their relationships to indiscretions, Bette apologizes for having ever judged Jenny about Marina:

Bette: *"I don't even know why you're talking to me about this. I mean, it wasn't like I was very nice to you when you went through all of this with Tim."*

Jenny: *"I don't know. I guess I know how that feels."*

L Is for . . .
Linking It Up

Title Card: Present Day, In Your Wildest Dreams

Alice is having a nightmare: She is in a jungle, typing on her laptop. We see that the screen is covered with a chant: "Dana is a friend of mine, she will do it anytime. For a nickel or a dime, 50 cents for overtime. Down the cellar she will go, she will strip from head to toe." Suddenly she is accosted by a tarted-up Tonya, who is clad in a vile, hot-pink mesh dress. Tonya rebukes her for being a bad girl. Alice looks frightened as she stares at Tonya's ample cleavage. Tonya proclaims to know all and, as she strokes her long red fingernail down Alice's chest, tells her that she's mad. "If you're gonna play, don't play without the Ton-Ton," she says to Alice, before grabbing her face and laying a huge, violent kiss on her resistant lips. Alice asks, "What about Dana?" Tonya shushes Alice and then directs her attention south, announcing, "Someone's hungry." Alice looks down and finds herself being eaten out by a rapacious and overly made-up Dana, who stares back up and says, "Starving!" Alice wakes up in her bed, at once startled and horrified.

The Link-up

At the party celebrating the reopening of The Planet, Tonya has a conversation with Alice on the dance floor that begins to feel like a confrontation. Alice worries Tonya is on to her about Dana, when she is actually apologizing to Alice for occupying so much of her best friend's time and attention. But as they are talking and dancing, Tonya and Dana are closing in on Alice, shimmying on either side of her. In a moment that distinctly echoes her dream, Tonya then drags her fingernail down Alice's chest, kneels in front of her, and says seductively, "Ton-Ton knows how to share."

Tony Salvatore, Ted "Mino" Gori). Shane recommends Carmen to Kit as a house DJ, which just might get her out of the doghouse with Señorita de la Pica Morales, where she's been put for her wanderlust. Tonya surprises Dana with a lunch filled with ad representatives from Absolut, Subaru, Adidas, Wilson, *Bride* magazine, the *Advocate*—all of whom have been invited to sponsor their upcoming wedding like a sporting event. What's creepier: The Ton-Ton is taking a 15 percent manager's fee from Dana's account to do it. The CAC needs sponsors for a new show, and Bette is relying on her failsafe source, the Peabody Foundation, to underwrite it. But Franklin has learned that Peggy just retired and relinquished her leadership of the foundation to her lesbian daughter, Helena. Jenny gets Charlotte Birch to reconsider her story after she passes her over for a seat in the exclusive master class. The fallout of Bette's and Tina's breakup reveals its impact on the others as Tina confesses to Alice that she's pregnant and has been withholding the information from Bette. A forlorn, dejected Miss Porter crashes a gathering at Jenny's and Shane's, appearing more drunken and melancholic by the minute.

BETTY

A veteran five-piece New York City–based group led by the songwriting trio Amy Ziff, Alyson Palmer and Elizabeth Ziff (Elizabeth is also known as "ez girl" and serves as *The L Word*'s composer), BETTY is the show's band on demand. For nearly twenty years, BETTY has been rocking across the country on stages, screens, and benefits for causes that are closest to their hearts: gay and lesbian rights, reproductive freedom, finding cures for breast cancer and AIDS. BETTY has written the new *L Word* theme song "The Way That We Live" (see lyrics on page 223), performing it at their live shows across the country. Most recently, they've been touring with their Off-Broadway hit *BETTY Rules!,* recording the show's score, and even making a few cameo appearances on the show.

Joyce Wischnia, played by Jane Lynch

Joyce Wischnia is a cigar-smoking, tough-talking successful civil rights lawyer who specializes in same-sex
marriage and divorce cases. Tina seeks her counsel
when she considers a separation agreement with Bette
to secure the baby's future. Joyce is well-intentioned
and is immediately drawn to Tina, but her arrogance
renders her unable to hear the word "no" when the
pregnant client rebuffs her unwelcome advances.

A fantastic comic actress, Jane Lynch has made
countless television guest appearances and film
cameos, but she is perhaps most beloved for her major roles in *Best in Show, A Mighty Wind,* and most
recently, *The 40 Year-Old Virgin.*

Ilene Chaiken on Breakup Fallout in the L World

"We really are family, and at the same time, we
have these very intricate, serpentine relationships in
which, because we're all women, both members of
a couple are friends with the entire group. It's not
quite so simple when the breakup happens. Often
with men and women breaking up, there's still that
who-gets-the-friends issue, but it's a little easier.
The guy has his friends, the girl has her friends, and
they pretty much remain intact. With a lesbian
breakup, sometimes it's very, very disruptive to the
group as a whole."

"Lynch Pin": Episode 204

Written by Ilene Chaiken
Directed by Lisa Cholodenko

The lesbian community may be insular, but not all lesbians are instant friends, as Bette learns the hard way when she goes to New York City to meet Helena Peabody and get a pulse on the status of the CAC's grant proposal. Helena is taking the Peabody Foundation in a new, humanitarian, less arts-oriented direction, seemingly determined to reject all of her mother's interests and allies out of spite, with Bette Porter at the top of her list. Bette is so desperate to save the Peabody funding, she crashes Peggy's massage at a private spa to beg her to intervene. Peggy refuses and instead gives Bette an eyeful of her and her new foreign lover

• Hollywood producer Veronica Bloom threatens the job of a prima donna actress on the set: "You tell her that if she's not back on that set in ten minutes with her hair perfect, I will fire her sorry ass and replace it with Kate Winslet's spotless mind!"

• Mark and Jenny bond over a mutual love of the Maysles brothers' documentary, *Grey Gardens*.

• When Tina rebuffs Joyce Wischnia's pass, the lawyer says, "Don't worry. I'll be careful. I've made love to a pregnant woman before."

• One of Shane's girlfriends offers this random piece of gossip while hanging out in the living room: "Liz Van Assum and Gabby Deveaux are like totally dressed in S/M leather. And Gabby? She has a huge chain from her crotch that goes through her legs and is padlocked to Liz's crotch."

171

Music featured in this episode:

"Today," Sweatshop Union

"Panis Angelicus," Franck

"Sofa Rockers," Kruder and Dorfmeister

"Goodtimes," Joystick

"Talk and Talk," The Cinch

"Pas Davantage," Brigitte Bardot

"Disco Blackout," Controller, Controller

"Lover's Spit," Broken Social Scene

"Naked as We Came," Iron and Wine

Bette's Art Collection:

Joyce Wischnia and Tina take inventory of Bette's artwork when she's in New York City. What does she have?

• In the dining room: *Day* by Lisa Yuskavage (on loan from the Marianne Boesky Gallery).

• In the living room: Oil paintings by Susan Anderson (*Glacier Sliver, Balcony Sliver, Pool Sliver, Golf Sliver*) and *Blue Channel* by Greg Murdock.

• In the bedroom: A color reproduction of video outtakes by Julia Scher.

• In the bathroom: A photograph, *Waking Eve,* by Dianne Whelan.

Dr. Benjamin Bradshaw, played by Charles S. Dutton

Dr. Benjamin Bradshaw is the author of *The Theory of Everything,* a self-help book based on Einstein's Theory of Relativity. Because he is constantly traveling around the country delivering lectures and giving seminars, Benjamin rarely sees his wife and kids in Portland, Oregon, and becomes instantly attracted to Kit after she attends one of his self-actualization seminars. She knows the score, but business at The Planet has never been better and neither has her self-confidence since meeting the doctor. No amount of emotional preparation can ease the pain when he returns to his wife as quickly as he came into her life.

Charles S. Dutton is an award-winning actor and director of stage and screen, who as a young man spent over seven years in jail for manslaughter before heading to Yale School of Drama. The star of several of August Wilson's plays, Dutton has most recently appeared in the films *Something the Lord Made* and *Secret Window,* and guest starred on the TV show *Without a Trace.*

getting a naked rubdown. Exasperated, Bette heads to the East Village gay club Starlight, where she spends her evening drinking martinis . . . and her night with a sexy little fawn she hooked up with in the bar. Tina and Joyce Wischnia take the opportunity to assess the value of Bette's art collection, while Joyce assesses the value of Tina's gratitude by making an unwelcome pass at her. Shane has lined up a potentially lucrative gig as an assistant to Veronica Bloom, the volatile head of a Hollywood studio, but it's not enough to bail her and Jenny out of their dire financial straits. They look for a third roommate, interviewing every nut in West Hollywood—a nudist, an aspiring starlet, a crazy proselytizing Christian who wants to "cure" their homosexuality—finally settling on an aggressive videographer named Mark Wayland, who persuades them with his ability to pay six months' rent-up front. When Mark informs Jenny that he can't read her sexuality based on her current looks, she has Shane cut off all of her hair—an emotionally charged scene that evokes Samson and Delilah, except that Jenny feels empowered with her tresses lopped off. Kit also seeks empowerment when she attends her first seminar with Dr. Benjamin Bradshaw, the author of a self-affirmation book called *The Theory of Everything.* It's official: Dana can't resist Alice. Watching the flirtatious exchanges between Alice and the guy that Tonya has brought for her is enough motivation for Dana to risk stealing a surreptitious snog in a public place.

L Is for . . .
Linking It Up

Title Card: New York City, Present Day

Helena Peabody is sitting across from her shrink, Dr. Isabel de Obaldia. They are talking about a transgression that took place in an earlier session in which Helena seduced her. Helena is taking off her jacket amid Dr. de Obaldia's protests. Helena is asking her why it is wrong to act on desire, while her shrink is arguing that as her doctor, she acted irresponsibly and could lose her license as a result. Helena slowly walks over to her and kisses her neck. Dr. de Obaldia initially resists, but soon they are ravishing each other.

The Link-up

This is the episode where Bette goes to New York to meet Helena. The opening vignette gives us a glimpse into Helena's psyche. Her psychiatric treatment has been corrupted by the one person she pays to trust, and she presumably goes to see Dr. de Obaldia to talk about her mother, Peggy, who has always bought her daughter's affections and rarely gives Helena the attention she craves. Judging by what we come to know about Helena, she has never experienced, or even witnessed, an example of a healthy relationship. This knowledge helps to explain why Helena is bossy, needy, and territorial with Tina—who is nurturing and kind—and threatened by Bette, who has won Peggy's affections.

Veronica Bloom, played by Camryn Manheim

Veronica Bloom is one of the hottest—and hottest-headed—producers in Hollywood. She is intrigued by Shane, whom she dubs "hair girl," because she admires her integrity and her unique ability to do what she can't: calm disquieted souls. She hires her as her assistant to close deals and soothe anything and anyone on demand. But no matter how broke she is, Shane has too much dignity to indulge Veronica's obnoxious whims and ultimately walks away from the job.

Camryn Manheim is an Emmy and Golden Globe award–winning actress for her role in *The Practice*. A memorable scene stealer, she's appeared in countless movies and television shows, among them *Romy and Michele's High School Reunion, Happiness, The Laramie Project,* and *Elvis,* the TV miniseries for which she was most recently nominated for an Emmy.

Katherine Moennig and Paul Edwards, key hair stylist, Discuss the Art of Fake Hair Cutting

Paul Edwards: When a haircut is written in the script, you have to spell it out for viewers. In life, people might go for a haircut, and they get a little trim and no one even notices. But on television, viewers have to be able to see it. The actor has to have some sort of obvious change. We just had a scene with Rosanna Arquette, where she comes to Shane for a haircut. Her hair's already long. I put in hair extensions so that when she goes into the shop, it's actually way longer than her own hair. When we took out her extensions and styled it up, it looks like she got a haircut.

Katherine Moennig: Paul is my hair guru. He taught me how to hold scissors and comb hair at the same time. I got a tutorial about how hair grows and which way, and was taught how to do the foil, which I had to do for Erin in the first season, when I gave her that makeover. The foil is easy—just another thing with hand motions. You have to learn how to do it with the comb and the scissors and make it look neat and professional. But I must admit that it gives me a little bit of anxiety during rehearsals because, between doing the scene and the lines and getting all motions down and giving it continuity, well, it's a lot at once. Imagine being on *ER*.

They shoot the scenes with the camera facing the person, and I stand behind her. So I go through the motions of combing and cutting the hair, but I am not actually touching the hair—I'm either just below the hair or right next to it. Once, during the first season, I was practicing fake-cutting the hair on this girl who also does hair on the show—she was my test dummy—and accidentally cut a big chunk of her hair. She was really cool about it. In season three, I give a girl a mohawk. Paul is teaching me to actually cut hair because they wanted me to really shave this girl's hair off. I gave Paul a mohawk. I must say, I gave him a really good mohawk.

Paul Edwards on the Haircutting Scene in "Lynch Pin"

"Originally, they wanted to shoot this scene from the back. I said, You have to shoot that from the front. Jenny knows she is getting her hair cut and how attached she is to her hair. Katherine's not a hairdresser. It was rigged, obviously. We put in all this fake hair that she had to chop away and you see it fall—it's very dramatic. Just at the moment that it's being cut, even as fake as it is, the drama of her hair being cut off is going to read all over her face. We need to see that. That scene is so many things: Jenny letting go of her past because Jenny at that point is like, I don't know what I'm doing, I don't know what's happening. At the same time, she's feeling like, Yeah I'm getting this haircut, but it's emotional and it's a thing that I'm supposed to do to be a lesbian. Later, she'll realize she doesn't need to do that to be who she is, and she'll grow her hair out, but for a brief time, it's like a rite of passage."

"Labyrinth": Episode 205
Written by Rose Troche
Directed by Burr Steers

The engagement party is coming up, and Alice finds herself on an excruciating jaunt to the local sex toy shop with Dana and Tonya, who dismisses her bisexuality as indecisiveness. But Alice doesn't appear very indecisive later on when she's yanking Dana's pants off during their gift-bag-stuffing session. It's Dana who seems torn at the engagement party as she watches two emotional speeches competing for her affections, one by her mother Sharon who gives Tonya her blessing, and the other by Alice, whose heartache over the spectacle is evident from the tears crackling through her voice. Tina reluctantly and temporarily moves back home, much to Bette's delight. She sees it as an opportunity to entice Tina back for good. The reunion plan gets derailed by the announcement of the Peabody Grant recipients: The CAC is passed over in favor of the Headquarters for Social Justice, whose proposal was written by Tina. What's worse, Helena Peabody, who is in from New York to personally congratulate Tina and announce the foundation's new agenda, connects the dots for Bette in a most humiliating way: Her ex's glow and weight gain indicate pregnancy. Veronica Bloom is self-aware enough to know she is charmless, so

This Is the Episode in Which . . .

• Jenny quips, "Mark, I think that there is a lot of 'I's' contradicting the 'we's' in your run-on sentence" in response to his request that she and Shane participate in his documentary on "bean-fiddlers" (Shane's word) and "bobbing-for-apple girls" (Jenny's word).

• Alice opts for the breast lollipop over the penis pop at the sex toy shop, answering Tonya and Dana's aggressive inquiry about her bisexuality.

• Veronica Bloom begs Shane to close a deal for her by following her around the driveway, barking from the top of her car: "Come on, Shane, Come on, come on! I got a present for ya, baby! Once we punch the deal, we can go get a mani-pedi. Come on! Come on, Shane. *Come on! Mwah!*"

• We meet Tonya's wonderfully tacky, incredibly supportive gay-positive parents.

• Sharon Fairbanks gets some long-overdue lesbian action: a lap dance at her daughter's engagement party.

• Helena crashes the engagement party as Tina's date, bringing expensive gifts to make up for her presence.

Music featured in this episode:

"Do You Take It?," The Wet Spots

"All My People," Kia Kadiri

"I Want You," Coco Love Alcorn

"Finally," CeCe Peniston

"Vamos Jogar," Sueca

"Fever," Coco Love Alcorn

"Just One Night," Coco Love Alcorn

"Get On," Dirtmitts

"Quiza Quiza Quiza," Peer

"Deceptive," Tandem/Nine

"Don't Go to Strangers," Etta Jones

"Moody," Tricky

she dispatches Shane to close a deal for the rights to the life story of a former prostitute who was mixed up with the Russian mob. Shane proves more effective as a closer than a matchmaker: Carmen balks at her attempts to set her up with Jenny, who she thinks is weird, even for a writer. Mark finds all of this fascinating, and his aggressive curiosity about lesbian life drives him to invade the living room with cameras and questions, offering Jenny, Shane, and their friends twenty dollars an interview for their troubles. What the women don't realize is that he and his friend Gomey (Sam Easton) are planting nine hidden cameras throughout the house to find out even more about them.

Erin Daniels says:

"The scene where Dana and Alice finally get together is one of my favorites. Director Burr Steers had been given an outline to work with, and Leisha and I pretty much made up all of it. We had attempted to make fun of our own clothes, because the clothes on the show are such a thing: the jeans that won't come off, and the shirt that gets caught, the beads. The clothes are so small. And then we did the whole *9 1/2 Weeks* send-up at the end. We just wanted to have fun with the scene, instead of making it this dramatic, sentimental moment, because that's who Dana and Alice are."

L Is for . . . Linking It Up

Title Card: Los Angeles, Present Day

Gomey is sitting at the information desk at a hotel. He is watching the security camera, a dopey grin on his face. He gasps, "Holy shit!" while gawping at a couple having sex in a stairwell and calls Mark to report what he sees.

The Link-up

Gomey gives Mark the idea to use hidden cameras for his new secret film project. The two of them hang the cameras all over the house, including in Jenny's and Shane's bedrooms. Mark's particular focus is Shane, whose prowess with women fascinates him. But as he watches her life play out, he becomes increasingly interested in her emotional life, which will eventually break up his friendship with Gomey. But that is nothing compared to the moment Jenny discovers the tapes. Mark is forced to face both Jenny and Shane, who are enraged by the violation.

"Lagrimas de Oro": Episode 206
Written by Guinevere Turner
Directed by Jeremy Podeswa

Helena starts to slither into Bette's sphere like a boa constrictor: She brings Leo Herrera (Warren Christie) in to the CAC as a fund raiser, directly threatening Bette's position there. And though Bette doesn't know it yet, Helena seduces Tina at the Chateau Marmont Hotel during the Peabody Grant recipient dinner. Kit enjoys a bit of room service, too, with her married self-help guru Dr. Benjamin Bradshaw, who is secretly taking their self-actualization workshops to more intimate settings. She does manage to convince Bette to attend one of her new man's seminars. Bette is initially resistant, but she ultimately follows Benjamin's advice on how best to approach Tina about their future as coparents and, hopefully, reunited partners when she learns that Tina used Marcus Allenwood's sperm. Alice refuses to be Dana's "backdoor woman" and demands that she leave Tonya after the Heineken Celebrity Slammin' Jammin' Tournament. Dana's dread is replaced by shock and hor-

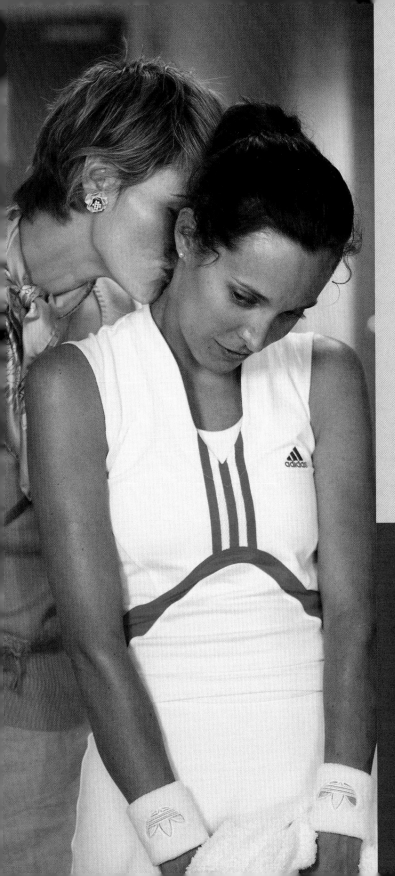

This Is the Episode in Which . . .

• Mark reveals his secret to getting laid: "I make a lot of eye contact, laugh at all their jokes. Oh, and what signs and seals the deal is I tell a tragic childhood story."

• Bette drives to Franklin's house late at night to ream him for hiring Leo Herrera.

• Jenny seeks out Charlotte while she's lifting weights at the gym, who tells her: "I'm not into the whole student-teacher transference thing. I prefer to keep the boundaries between us crisp and clear." At that moment, Jenny's classmate Hunter Kirby walks up to Charlotte, and spots her with a barbell.

• Charlotte gives Jenny a "silence" assignment.

• Melissa Rivers tells Dana, "I like to think of myself as label-free. I mean, love is love and I've fallen in love with Tonya the person, not the gender."

Music featured in this episode:

"Hit Me with Your Best Shot,"
 Pat Benatar

"The Vanishing," Stars

"Back 2 Love," Kia Kadiri

"Chocolate Cake," Paloma

"Kemence Dance," 5 Alarm

"Life Is Long When You're Lonely,"
Monistir

"Gold Digger," Hipjoint

"Playgirl," Ladytron

"Allegro Moder," Schubert

L Is for . . . Linking It Up

Title Card: Los Angeles, Present Day

Kit and Dr. Benjamin Bradshaw are having lunch at a hotel poolside café. He is explaining how he doesn't normally socialize with his students, but he's been feeling so lonely being away from his wife and children for months at a time. Their conversation becomes more personal as they bond over the loneliness of traveling—Kit remembers it from her days touring with her band. After lunch, they walk out of the hotel together for an awkward, intimate good-bye: his cautious kisses on her cheek turn into a serious lip-lock. She stops him to consider her next move. The next shot is of a fully clothed Kit and Benjamin kissing passionately on a hotel room bed.

The Link-up

Kit and Benjamin begin a passionate affair that proves to be Kit's healthiest relationship to date, despite his marital status. She moves forward with him with both eyes open and even introduces him to her father, Melvin, who immediately takes to him. But all the emotional preparation in the world doesn't make her feel any less bereft when he eventually returns to his family.

ror when her teary breakup speech is foiled by her fiancée's news that she has unexpectedly fallen in love with Melissa Rivers (who appears as herself). Carmen and Jenny make romantic overtures toward each other, but Shane proves to be a distraction. Jenny imagines an exquisite fantasy, casting Charlotte as a circus announcer, Carmen as a temptress, and Shane as a temptress tamer. Jenny is a lone tortured ballerina who falls to her death when she sees the tamer and temptress making out in the arena. Mark has his own insights into the unfolding drama between his two roommates and Carmen, though he is most drawn to Shane, who is as caddish with women as she is charismatic. He sends her a flower delivery girl, and then watches the action on his video monitor with Gomey.

Melissa Rivers, as herself

Melissa Rivers, daughter of acerbic veteran comedienne Joan Rivers, is hosting the Heineken Celebrity Slammin' Jammin' Tournament, and to Tonya's mind, the *E! Red Carpet* cohost *is* the celebrity of whom Heineken speaks. So starstruck is Tonya by Melissa Rivers (she first chases her down at the "Provocations" opening in "Limb from Limb") that she blows off her engagement to Dana. Too bad Dana didn't let Tonya speak first—Dana agonized over her Dear Jane speech, crying as she tried to break it to her gently. Imagine her surprise when Tonya and Melissa lock lips right in front of her, the creep factor undermining the emotional power of her heartfelt words.

Heike Brandstatter and Coreen Mayrs, Casting say:

"We were trying to pick the person whom Tonya would have the affair with. They wanted a famous tennis star to be caught making out with a famous tennis star in the locker room—just a scene, though, there's no dialogue. They had a list of people, and at the top of it was Martina Navratilova," says Heike Brandstatter.

"As time went on, it became apparent that we probably weren't going to get a famous tennis star. We were doing another movie at the time, *Confessions of a Sociopathic Social Climber,* and Melissa Rivers was in that film," recalls Coreen Mayrs. "I phoned the producer and said, 'Weird idea, but do you think Melissa Rivers would want to play a lesbian on *The L Word*?' He asked her and she said, 'Sure.' In the next casting session with Ilene, I told her I had an idea for this character, Melissa Rivers, and everyone on the couch was confused. But Ilene thought it was hilarious. It was funny because she's playing herself, and she was a lesbian. I think they should bring Melissa Rivers back!"

Director Jeremy Podeswa says:

"As a director, you are given license to do almost anything. The way Jenny's fantasy was written into the script in a way that was more literary and not so cinematic. The purpose of the fantasy as written was to actually say something about Jenny that I felt had already been said in other episodes. So I talked with Ilene about changing the concept of it a little bit so that it would be more specific to what she was going through in this episode. Stylistically I did my own thing with it and made it very different than other Jenny fantasies. It was really fun to do.

"The scene between Laurel and Rachel [having sex] in the pool felt like we were doing something unique and kind of amazing. Laurel was incredibly game, and she made Rachel as comfortable as she could be. Laurel is so comfortable with herself that it made it all so possible. But it was funny because when you know there's something so matter-of-fact about doing it that you sort of forget at some point that it can be something a little bit shocking. I thought it was really tasteful, but the idea of it and the frankness of it—in some ways the boldness of it—can be shocking to some people, I guess. I got no negative feedback at all when the show aired, and I think the initial reaction was anticipating somebody's fear of the way other people might react, like I don't know if people are ready for this. But people are ready for a lot of things. It didn't create even a ripple when it aired as far as I know."

Ricardo Spinacé, Production Design says:

"I love the set we did for the circus in Jenny's fantasy. We did that scene indoors at Stage Two, and the place was just packed with the CAC, Alice's apartment, and Jenny's bedroom. We were going to do this outdoors, but I thought that it was going to rain, and I was worried that the wind would blow the tent off. I didn't need a whole tent, just a half of a tent. I decided to make it inside. I went to our producer and said I think I can make it inside, and he said, What? Where? I showed him drawings and worked with the construction, and we over-realized it, with large stripes, which made it seem like a much larger tent. I went all the way up to the rafters and it worked."

"Luminous": Episode 207
Written by Ilene Chaiken
Directed by Ernest Dickerson

Dana and Alice finally get out of bed long enough to officially announce their relationship at an evening gathering at The Planet. Helena is having a hard time keeping her hands off Tina, even when her young children, Jun Ying and Wilson, unexpectedly burst into the room, which unsettles her pregnant girlfriend. Tina is more uncomfortable, however, witnessing Helena's battles with her ex, Winnie Mann, over the custody of their children. At least they lend Tina some insight on how to proceed with Bette. Leo shows up at the CAC, and in the same breath he uses to assure Bette about respecting her position, he mentions running into Helena and Tina,

This Is the Episode in Which . . .

• Veronica Bloom says, "You want me to go from Marty to M. Night-fucking-Shyamalan? Where were you educated? Do you even know the difference between *War and Peace* and a Marvel fucking comic book?!"

• Bette meets sculptor Leigh Ostin at a studio visit. She goes to check her out and is nearly as smitten with the artist as she is with her blown-glass mobiles—she buys one. Bette invites Leigh and her girlfriend, Valerie, to join her at The Planet to see Sharon Isbin perform.

• Winnie Mann first meets Tina as she's being eaten out by Helena on the patio.

Music featured in this episode:

"Meditation for Sarah," Elizabeth Ziff

"Cartoon Music," Amazing Stranger

"Zapateado," performed live by Sharon Isbin

"Magic Man," Bonobo

"Smile and Beware," Girl Nobody

"Mmmnn," Grandadbob

"Number 1," Natasha Thirsk

"Where Do I Begin? (Away Team Remix)," Shirley Bassey

"The Other Girl," The Capitals

"Apology," Nasty On

"Coming Back to You," Leonard Cohen

Winnie Mann, played by Melissa Leo

Winnie Mann is a New York City–based playwright and the ex-partner of Helena Peabody. She is also the birth mother of their son, Wilson, and is suing Helena for custody of him and their adopted daughter, Jun Ying. She appeals to Bette to testify as a character witness against Helena.

Melissa Leo was in the cast of the television series *Homicide: Life on the Streets,* has guest starred on *Law & Order: Criminal Intent,* and *CSI: Crime Scene Investigation,* and has recently appeared in such movies as *American Gun, 21 Grams,* and the upcoming Henry Jaglom film *Hollywood Dreams.*

who appear excited about their imminent parenthood. At least Bette's luck is changing: She gets "meat-tagged" at The Planet by a stream of available women when Tina tells her she is ready to discuss her place in the baby's life. Charlotte grudgingly compliments Jenny by referring her for a ghostwriting job for her movie star friend Burr Connor. Veronica is on a tear when a major director drops out of her project, so she drags Shane along on her spa day. Shane is barely able to stomach watching Veronica get a chemical peel, but she gets a complimentary bottle of OxyContin for her troubles. She draws the line at spending the evening with her in bed popping Xanax and watching *Funny Girl*, and flees Veronica's mansion as the Hollywood powerhouse hurls insults and threats at her. But the sight of Jenny and Carmen together at The Planet, and then in their kitchen, isn't making her day any better. Shane tries to numb it all with a pair of sexy twins and a night of snorting Oxy, while Jenny confronts Carmen in the other room, forcing her to acknowledge her feelings for her roommate. The next morning, Carmen rips into the hungover heartbreaker about her total disregard of everyone's feelings, which is the final straw for Shane, who goes on a self-destructive spree that ultimately requires a rescue mission by Mark.

"Loyal": Episode 208
Written by A. M. Homes
Directed by Alison Maclean

Mark is getting pressure from his pal Gomey and their slimy boss, Eric, about his lesbian documentary, which they worry is getting arty and sentimental, and veering too far away from the nether regions. If he fails to deliver, Mark will be forced to pay back every dime he's been advanced. Jenny worries she lost a lucrative opportunity when she boasts about her girlfriend to closeted movie star Burr Connor during their job interview. Alice's ongoing honeymoon with Dana distracts her from coming up with radio show ideas for her upcoming audition with KCRW. A visit to The Planet lends some inspiration when she runs into Gabby Deveaux and her new girlfriend, Lara Perkins, who has just been hired as the new chef. The weird encounter leads to a spontaneous and inadvertent Chart rant, which strikes exactly the right tone to the ears of KCRW's producers. Tina is increasingly torn between two lovers: She invites Bette to her sonogram appointment, and agrees to accompany Helena on a house hunt. The friends are finding their sympathies tipping in Bette's favor, foregoing Helena's housewarming party invitation and instead visiting Bette, who appears

This Is the Episode in Which . . .

• Bette tells Tina she is planning to get back into therapy with Dan Foxworthy.

• Bette outshines Leo and Helena at a CAC board meeting, where they are aggressively courting elusive artist Allen Barnes to host her retrospective. Barnes is impressed by Bette's authoritative knowledge of her work, with Bette distinctly recalling her graduate thesis, which focused on Barnes's work and was excerpted in *Artforum*.

• On the day of her KCRW interview, Alice and Dana discover that both of their bodies are covered with hickeys. Helena gives Alice a vintage Hermès scarf to cover them up.

• Mark explains the Samurai code to Shane and offers himself up as her servant.

• Upon hearing of her run-in with Gabby Deveaux, Dana tells Alice, "I don't necessarily think we should be friends with our exes."

Music featured in this episode:

"Ship That Died of Shame," Nasty On

"Pastures of Heaven," Ridley Bent

"Get Back at It," East Mezzo

"Mahk Jchi," Ulali

"Dolls & Bennies," BETTY

"Les Cheveaux de Mon Amor," Lola Dutronic

"Tell Me Again," Ron Sexsmith

Burr Connor, played by Tony Goldwyn

Burr Connor is a 1980s film action star who ruined the life of his costar Rod Sebring, with whom he was madly in love, by planting career-damaging stories about his homosexuality when he found him screwing around with other guys. He lives his life in romantic solitude, paying people hush money to keep quiet about his homosexuality for fear that being outed will end his lucrative career. Burr and Jenny briefly discuss the possibility of a literary collaboration when Charlotte Birch suggests he hire her as a ghostwriter for his memoir. In a moment of weakness, he discloses his carefully guarded secret and then fires Jenny for fear that she'll convince him to include it in the book.

Tony Goldwyn is a renowned actor and a director, who has played on both sides of the camera for *The L Word*, as well as on the TV series *Without a Trace*. He has appeared in films such as *Romance & Cigarettes*, *Bounce*, and *Ghost*, guest starred on *Frasier*, *Murphy Brown*, and *Designing Women*, and directed the films *A Walk on the Moon*, *Someone Like You*, and the upcoming *The Last Kiss*, which features Lauren Lee Smith, otherwise known as Lara the "soup chef."

grateful for the company. Helena tightens the CAC noose around Bette's neck by joining the steering committee. Bette has gotten a few points on how to handle Helena from Winnie Mann, who has asked her to testify as a character witness at their children's custody trial. Carmen confronts Shane about her profound fear of intimacy. When Shane seeks counsel from a priest, we learn that Shane's skittishness comes from a lifetime of abandonment beginning at nine, when her drug-addicted mother left her in foster care.

L Is for . . .
Linking It Up

Title Card:
On Location with
Burr Connor, 1985,
Lone Pine, California

Two cowboys, one played by Burr Connor, the second by Rod Sebring, are rushing up a rocky path, followed by a woman in a petticoat and a hat. The second cowboy rebukes the first for bringing the woman along because he claims she is slowing them down. The first cowboy says, "Sometimes a man's gotta do what a man's gotta do." The camera pans back to reveal they are on a live film shoot.

Next we see Burr Connor emerging from his trailer dressed in his street clothes. The trailer next to his is rumbling. He goes in and finds Rod Sebring and another man having sex. He pulls the man off of Rod and throws him out. The man is naked and he crashes on the pavement. Burr lambastes Rod for being indiscreet, telling him that he has "too much riding on this picture."

The Link-up

Jenny is gearing up for her first meeting with Burr Connor by hosting a private film festival with Carmen, who is a huge fan of his Westerns. Jenny picks up a homoerotic vibe from the films, and senses a deep love between the two leading men, Burr and Rod. She and Burr get along well enough until she mentions having a girlfriend. He decides not to hire her because her lesbianism makes him uncomfortable. Charlotte Birch is annoyed by his squeamishness and implores him to give Jenny another chance. The two bond, and this time he spills his guts: Rod Sebring was the love of his life. Burr sabotaged his career. And, by his own admission, he's too cowardly to come out of the closet. And then he fires Jenny for fear that she will slip it into his memoir.

"Late, Later, Latent": Episode 209
Written by David Stenn
Directed by Tony Goldwyn

Charlotte Birch gets Burr to reconsider Jenny's writing services after arranging lunch for the three of them. The movie star and his ghostwriter bond when Jenny turns up at his mansion in tears after inadvertently discovering two connected betrayals at home—Mark's cache of videotapes, which includes an intimate and revelatory conversation between Carmen and Shane about their true feelings for each other—while Burr confides that he's gay and terrified of coming out. His subsequent disclosure means he can't hire her because he doesn't want to be exposed. Eric and Gomey are infuriated with Mark when he shows them the finished cut of *A Compendium of Lesbianism, Volume I,* which he hopes will make it to Sundance. He is promptly fired, and now has to pay Eric back all the money he fronted him. Veronica Bloom and Shane face off for the last time when the Hollywood producer anonymously hires the stylist to do her hair for her profile in the *New York Times Magazine.* After her sonogram

This Is the Episode in Which . . .

- After she sleeps with Tina, Bette confesses to Dan Foxworthy that she "lost her. She doesn't belong to me anymore. It feels like someone else had been touching her and making love to her and I *felt* that other person and I felt her connection to that other person, you know? And she did things that we had never done together. And it was like she was so free."

- Dana is concerned that Alice's dildo campaign is really masking her bisexual desires: "You're trying to have your cake and eat your pussy too . . . because, wait. I don't wanna do that with you. I mean, if you're trying to make me into a man because you think that there's something missing . . ." Alice allays Dana's anxieties when she explains that "many bonafide lesbians find strapping it on the ultimate way of fucking. And I think it'd be really hot for you to fuck me like that."

Music featured in this episode:

"Succexy," Metric

"Bring It On," Kia Kadiri

"Walking Backwards," Transientworld

"Send Me You," The Butchies

"No Other Love," Heart

"Red Licorice," Maggie Moore

"El Cumbanchero," Mambo Allstars

"Lay Around," Jealous Girlfriends

193

L Is for . . . Linking It Up

Title Card: Los Angeles, This Morning

Carmen and Jenny are in the shower together. Jenny gets out and goes to the toilet to urinate. Carmen follows her and straddles her on the toilet. She tells Jenny to spread her legs wider and then they urinate together. Mark is pacing outside the bathroom. He tells Shane that they're taking forever. She bangs on the door, and when they don't respond, Shane bursts in on Carmen and Jenny going at it. The three of them freeze, with Shane and Jenny looking especially embarrassed. Shane closes the door and tells Mark to use the bushes.

The Link-up

Shane and Carmen have a clandestine and intimate conversation in the kitchen that is secretly being filmed and viewed by Mark. Shane admits to Carmen that it's "hard for me to have you and Jenny in my face all the time." Carmen tells her that she is in a holding pattern until the real deal comes along, and that real deal is Shane. Carmen dismisses Shane's questions about Jenny, telling her, "Jenny wouldn't know what the real deal was if it bit her in the ass. She is so lost in her own darkness. I think she likes it in there." Carmen's words seem to break through to Shane because she appears to be on the verge of kissing her.

When Jenny goes to retrieve her Burr Connor DVDs from Mark's studio, she discovers his vast library of surveillance tapes. She watches the "Shane/Carmen Love Confession" tape, and begins to weep when she hears Carmen's harsh words about her.

appointment, Tina slowly invites Bette back into her life, at least as far as her bed for now: The two make love for the first time since their breakup. In turn, Bette sets up a nursery in her house for the baby in hopes that Tina will move back home. Helena also has an exquisite nursery awaiting Tina's new baby, which she shows her during their intimate dinner date, a gesture of apology for abandoning Tina in the grips of her hormonal meltdown the day before. Bette dedicates herself to self-improvement, returning to therapy and finally articulating her newfound respect for Kit and her thriving business. But Kit almost gets derailed when Benjamin cancels their dinner at the last minute to be with his wife. She reconnects with Ivan at an AA meeting, only to feel betrayed when she learns that he's been hiding a crucial fact of his life—he's had a girlfriend for the past five years. And Dana finally gets over her dildo apprehension and goes sex toy shopping with Alice—and surprises her later when she decides to test-drive the strap-on.

"Land Ahoy": Episode 210
Written by Ilene Chaiken
Directed by Tricia Brock

Jenny confronts Mark about the "rape-y cameras," but orders him not to utter a word to Shane and Carmen until they return from their vacation with Dana, who is bringing them along when she is invited as a guest panelist on an Olivia cruise. Mark's violation of their privacy triggers vague but haunting memories of a long-repressed trauma in Jenny's life, and, absconding with one of his video cameras, she begins a new project exploring her family's history with violence and mental illness. She betrays nothing of the Mark situation to Shane and Carmen, but she does act weirder than usual, orchestrating situations that might force the two women to admit their feelings to each other—and to her. Airport security has a field day with Dana's bags, which are stuffed with brand-new sex toys. But as she and Alice put them to the test in their reenactment of *The Love Boat,* they both wish they'd remem-

This Is the Episode in Which . . .

• Dana is a guest on *The Chart* and nearly hijacks Alice's show, sparking their first tiff.

• Mark warns Shane, "You're liable to hear shit about me while you're gone, and since I won't be there to defend myself, I just don't want you to think I'm a total asshole."

• Helena buys Tina a $5,000 evening gown to wear at the Peabody dinner.

• Dana and Alice get dragged to the Olivia cruise captain's table for dinner, while clad in their *Love Boat* costumes. And Dana is packing nine inches of pure latex heat.

• Phoebe Sparkle swears Shane to secrecy about their chaste sleepover.

L Is for . . . Linking It Up

Title Card: Key West, Florida

The sun is setting. A cellist is performing on a ship to an all-female audience. One woman, sexpert Phoebe Sparkle, is watching intently. Two women quietly argue over who will ask her their sex questions. One finally poses her question to Phoebe, who gives them an answer and then shushes them. When the cellist finishes her piece, Phoebe applauds her and makes a verbal pass at her. Cut to a series of scenes with Phoebe pleasuring the cellist in various locations on the ship: in her cabin (with a gaggle of women listening by the door), in a Jacuzzi, by the railing on the deck.

The Link-up

Dana has been invited as a guest on an Olivia cruise and brings along Alice, Jenny, Carmen, and Shane. Jenny has confronted Mark about the cameras and implores him to keep mum about it because she doesn't want him to ruin Shane's vacation. Jenny can't shake the Carmen and Shane conversation from her head and behaves strangely as a result. She becomes fixated on the idea of having a ménage à trois with Shane and Carmen—anything to get the two of them together and confess to Jenny their love for each other. When Shane is propositioned by Phoebe Sparkle, she feels temporarily relieved of the drama and gladly accepts. But the two women quickly discover that they are sexually incompatible: both Shane and Phoebe are tops. Shane can't bear to return to her claustrophobic cabin and instead crashes on Phoebe's couch.

Music featured in this episode:

"Cello Keys," performed live by Amy Ziff

"Salaam," Social Deviantz

"Sadness," Transientworld

"Big Ten Inch Record," Bull Moose Jackson

"BE '62," Chris Gestrin

"Let's Sick on the Decks," Grandadbob

"Erectangle Suite," Panurge

"On the Verge," Le Tigre

"Shadows Reflection," Allison Miller

"Sunny Came Home" performed live by Shawn Colvin

"Arabesque," Tony Salvatore

"Givin It to You," Coco Love Alcorn

"Restaurant Jazz 7," Amazing Stranger

bered to pack some Dramamine. Bette's visit with Melvin is more difficult than usual when he refuses to sympathize with her, or even acknowledge her breakup with Tina, which becomes more hurtful when he reaches out to Kit's new lover, Benjamin Bradshaw, despite the fact that he is married. At Helena's invitation, Bette attends the Peabody dinner honoring Tina for her community service. Tina tells Bette she'd like for them to start dating. But when Tina receives her award, she is disappointed to see that Bette has left the ceremony; that is, until she learns that Bette was called away to the hospital, where Melvin has been diagnosed with inoperable advanced prostate cancer. Shane, Carmen, and Jenny return home to a living room filled with dismantled cameras and labeled videos. Now that everything is out in the open, Jenny ends her relationship with Carmen, while Shane, who is awestruck by the sheer volume and detail of the tapes, breaks down and weeps before punching Mark in the face.

"Loud and Proud": Episode 211

Written by Elizabeth Hunter
Directed by Rose Troche

It's Gay Pride 2005, and Shane is feeling profoundly ashamed as she watches Mark's tapes, wondering aloud to Jenny if she really is as horrible as she appears. While the tapes serve as a wake-up call for Shane, the fact of them unhinges Jenny, who is retreating into herself in an effort to retrieve a deeply buried memory that may be the key to so much of her anguish. Bette is grappling with Melvin's decision to refuse medical treatment, as his mortality bears down on her. Despite her father's illness, Bette refuses to indulge his homophobia and demands some answers about the way he betrayed her mother

This Is the Episode in Which . . .

- After watching Mark's cache of tapes, Shane seeks out Jenny to tell her, "This is my home, Jenny. And for the first time, I actually have a room of my own. That's a huge thing for me. And I'm sorry. I am. I am sorry about what you saw on that tape. But I like living with you. I love it. I think we have a great time. All right? I just don't want to lose it."

- Alice has words with the organizer of the Gay and Lesbian Center float for not allowing her to ride on the float with Dana. She tells the organizer: "Well, it's not like it's the HRC or the GLAAD float or anything, anyway."

- Helena starts dating sculptor Leigh Ostin, who has recently broken up with her girlfriend, Valerie.

- Shane musters the courage to disclose several personal facts about her life to Carmen, indicating that she is ready to give intimacy a go.

199

L Is for . . . Linking It Up

Title Card: Los Angeles, Present Day

A female sex slave is gagged, chained, and bound to an X-shaped cross in a dark room in an S&M dungeon. Aimee is taunting her with a whip, slapping it across her stomach and then removing the gag to kiss her, rubbing the whip handle against her crotch until the sex slave is begging Aimee to fuck her. Aimee instead puts the gag back into the woman's mouth and leaves the dungeon. The sign on the door of the establishment reads: "Pride 2005 Celebrate Your Diversity.

The Link-up

After the Gay Pride parade, Alice and Dana walk by the dungeon and consider checking out a seminar on the seven stages of the cross, which include whipping, temporary piercing, public humiliation, anal penetration, and torching. Neither is interested in the sadomasochism, but both are tempted by the promise of a free buffet. They go in to check it out, and quickly walk out of the dungeon within seconds. Later, Jenny goes into the dungeon, where she offers herself up for a whipping on the leatherbound cross. The act of being bound conjures a disturbing flashback to her childhood of being held down and attacked by a group of young boys in the woods. We see a young dirty and tear stained] Jenny, looking blankly at the tents outside of a carnival, where a group of ultra Orthodox Jews are dancing and singing.

and his inability to accept Bette as she is. Melvin's illness heightens Tina's awareness of her connection to Bette, and she subsequently tells Helena of her decision to see Bette again. Mark begs Jenny's forgiveness, but she denies him and instead challenges him to remain in the house and face the consequences of his actions, making it very clear that her invitation is not a friendly gesture; he accepts. Alice is worried that Dana isn't taking their relationship as seriously as she is when Alice's declarations of love fail to provoke a response. But Dana is pretty distracted when her younger brother, Howie, inexplicably crashes their Gay Pride celebration. He finally spells it out for everyone when Dana finds him guzzling Cosmopolitans and dancing topless with a gay man at The Planet's big Pride bash by the end of the day: Homosexuality runs in the Fairbanks family. He's just hoping his big sister will help him come out to their parents.

"L'Chaim": Episode 212
Written by Ilene Chaiken
Directed by John Curran

Jenny is on the verge of a nervous breakdown as she tries to get a grasp on the child-hood memory that is haunting her and takes a job stripping at the Howling Coyote. She doesn't tell anyone about the gig, but she does invite Dana, Shane, Alice, and Carmen to meet her at the bar. As the men in the audience get rowdier and klezmer music begins to blare over the loudspeaker, she starts to recall flashes of images that become increasingly vivid; they depict the famous neo-Nazi rally in Skokie. Against Kit's advice, Bette decides to bring Melvin to her home to care for him until his death. She prepares the living room for him, replacing her artwork with family photos including a discreet picture of her and Tina to-gether. As Bette braces herself to say good-bye to her father in this home, she hopes it will also be the place where she has the opportunity to welcome a new life. Franklin offers Bette a leave of absence, but she worries that he might seize the opportunity to buy her out of her contract and put Leo in her stead. Before he passes away, Melvin lends some insight and advice about

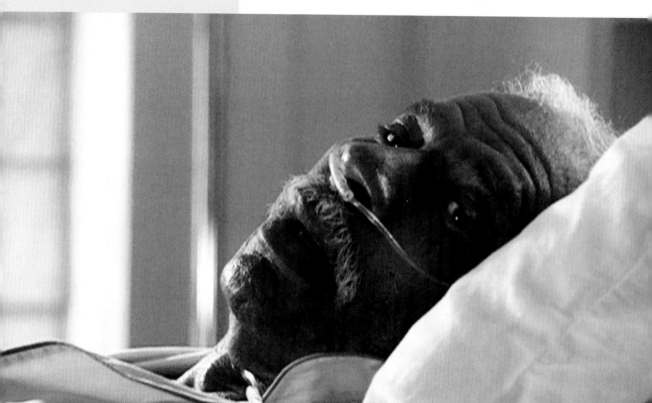

This Is the Episode in Which . . .

- As Tina strokes Bette's hair in front of a half-sleeping Melvin, he tells her to "promise to take care of my little girl." Bette believes they've had their long-awaited breakthrough, so she is devastated seconds later when she realizes he has mistaken Tina for Bette's mother.

- In a state of full consciousness, Melvin finally addresses Tina by her first name and not "Miss Kennard."

- Jenny shuts Mark out with her aggressive brand of the silent treatment.

- Mark and Shane go on an emergency errand for Bette to pick up liquid food for Melvin. Shane philosophizes: "It's the cycle of life: You wind up eating baby food and you're back in diapers!"

love, infidelity, and his regrets about the woman he believes he hurt the most: Bette's mother. Alice is unnerved when she and Dana run into a now-single Lara Perkins at The Planet. But she is nearly pushed over the edge when the two exes make plans to have dinner, terrified that they'll fall back in love. Helena is hoping that Tina will be jealous when she sees her out with Leigh Ostin, but imminent birth and death weigh far more heavily on Tina's mind and heart. Shane is changing her ways, opting out of a bump-and-grind spectacle with Peaches during her show at The Planet to instead seek out Carmen on the dance floor.

Music featured in this episode:

"B's," Othello 9

"Last Days," Brougham Camp

"I U She," performed live by Peaches

"Soul of a Man," Maria Muldaur

"Siyabobona," Kholeho Mosola

"Readie 2 Partie," MMO

"Happy," Touched

"Rusty Old Halo," Bob Merrill, sung by Bette and Kit

L Is for . . . Linking It Up

Title Card:
Los Angeles, Present Day

Jenny walks into a strip club called the Howling Coyote during the daytime. Aimee, the woman who bound and whipped her at Gay Pride, is waiting for her and calls out to a man named Victor to announce that Jenny has arrived. Victor looks at Jenny, shrugs his shoulders, and says, "Yeah, so?" Aimee says, "Trust me, she's a very sick girl." Jenny cracks a sly, slightly proud grin.

The Link-up

Jenny begins her stint as a stripper at the Howling Coyote and summons her friends to come for her debut performance as a naughty little yeshiva girl. Being on that stage, surrounded by rowdy, howling men, is at once cathartic and self-destructive: The experience helps conjure Jenny's repressed memories of her rape, but it is also propelling her toward a mental breakdown.

"Lacuna": Episode 213
Written by Ilene Chaiken
Directed by Ilene Chaiken

This somber episode revolves around Melvin Porter's funeral, which also doubles, in part, as *The L Word*'s memorial tribute to the actor who portrayed him: Ossie Davis died on February 4, 2005, three months before this episode aired. Feminist icon Gloria Steinem is among the attendants at the funeral—according to Bette, she and Melvin were old friends. At the reception, Steinem begins a lively discussion about sexuality and the state of feminism in the twenty-first century with Carmen, Jenny, Shane, Dana, Alice, and members of BETTY. Later Alice spies Dana flirting with Lara and forces her hand by suggesting they move in together. The pressure from Alice exacerbates Dana's skittishness, which further heightens Alice's anxiety, propelling an ever-worsening cycle that dooms their relationship, which Alice is already starting to mourn. She knows that she not only stands to lose her lover but her best friend and, quite possibly, her sanity. Franklin tells Bette what she has long been anticipating, and the timing couldn't be

Music featured in this episode:

"Cementhead," Tony Galla

"Ah Comme Bella a Stagione," Tony Galla

"Say Hallelujah," Tracy Chapman

"Voi Che Sapete," Mozart

"Ballad of the Broken Word," Toshi Regon

"L'ombre et La Lumière," Coralie Clement

"TKO," Le Tigre

"Kissing You," BETTY

"Buttons," Kinnie Starr

"Crazy on You," performed live by Heart

"Esta Noche," Federico Aubele

"Testimony," Sweet Honey in the Rock

more inappropriate: The CAC wants to buy out her contract and replace her with Leo Herrera. At least some poetic justice is served when Helena meets her mother for lunch and finds Peggy sitting with Winnie and the kids. Mama Peabody is not happy to hear of her daughter's bad temper. The drama moves over to the Gloria Project at the Wiltern Theatre, where Shane has begun her first proper date with Carmen, a romantic evening in which she finally tells her how much she loves her. Tina's water breaks at the theater before the event begins. She is forced to change her plans for a home birth at Bette's house when serious complications arise, and she almost dies. Next door, Jenny feels herself fracturing, much like the piece of broken mirror she uses to slice up her leg. Shane gets home just in time to stanch the bleeding and soothe Jenny's aching soul. She also delivers life-affirming news: Tina had her baby, and both are healthy. Later, Shane and Jenny join the others at the hospital to meet and welcome the newest member of their family: baby Angelica.

This Is the Episode in Which . . .

• James is forced to betray his loyalty to his boss when Helena threatens his job: She gets him to divulge Bette's whereabouts.

• On her way to her last prenatal ob-gyn appointment, Tina is accosted by Helena, who tries to strong-arm her into having lunch with her and her mother.

• Dana asks her new trainer, Lucia Rijker, "Why can't I just be a second-rate tennis player who's famous for being a lesbian?"

• Peggy is blown away by the level of lesbodrama that has been playing out between Helena, Leigh, Tina, and Bette.

• Peggy says, "I hope you girls write fabulous, sick, neurotic, tortured love poems to one another." Bette quips, "I'm actually working on several right now." Peggy responds, "Send me one, would you, Bette?"

• Jenny goes crazy on Heart, when they perform "Crazy on You" at The Wiltern.

Gloria Steinem, as herself

Feminist icon and founder of *Ms.* magazine Gloria Steinem appears as herself in the season finale, attending her old friend Melvin Porter's funeral. She has a round-table discussion about sexuality and feminism with Jenny, Carmen, Shane, Dana, Alice, and the women from BETTY and appears again later in the episode hosting a music benefit for the Ms. Foundation with special musical guests Heart, Kinnie Starr, and BETTY.

L Is for . . .
Linking It Up

Title Card: Sunset Strip, Present Day

We see a nighttime shot of the strip club where Jenny dances. The walls are adorned with neon-lit silhouettes of naked women. Inside, Jenny is stripping. The shouts of the crowd are muted. We are privy to Jenny's psyche as she works. A catalog of images flicker in her mind as she flings another article of clothing at the audience: her drawings of shouting men in Skokie; Carmen, the many-armed temptress; her young attacker in his clown shirt; young Jenny sitting in the shooting gallery; young Jenny and a friend shooting at her present-day self. Jenny slides her hands in her underwear and rubs herself before pulling off her panties and hurling them at the crowd. She stretches her arms out and arches her back like a champion Olympic gymnast before closing her eyes and holding her head in her hands as if to offer up her body like a sacrificial lamb. Her body appears to be detached from her soul.

The Link-up

Shane waits for Jenny outside the club after seeing her performance. She is concerned about Jenny's destructive behavior, and her choice to use striptease as a way to gain access to her repressed memories. Jenny asserts that it not only helps conjure memories but to seize power by controlling men's libidos through manipulation. She tells Shane, "When I'm in there, it's my fucking choice when I take off my top and I wanna show my breasts. And it's my fucking choice when I take off my pants and I show my pussy. And then I stop when I wanna stop and it makes me feel good because I'm in charge." Shane implores her to be safe, but later in the episode Shane returns home to find Jenny in the bathroom, bleeding profusely from self-inflicted cuts on her leg.

Looking Behind the Curtain
The L Crew

Creating lesbodrama is a long process that goes far beyond putting beautifully made-up women in gorgeous couture before the camera. *The L Word* needs its writers, directors, producers, set and production designers, location scouts, film editors, and postproduction and musical supervisors to set all of this drama in motion. In this section, we meet some of the people who stir the pot and boil it all down into episodes we can't stop watching.

Leading the Crew: Rose Lam, Executive Producer

As the person in charge of production, Rose Lam is like a troubleshooter and an air-traffic controller rolled into one, watching over every department from costumes to casting, making sure everyone is on the same page of the same book. She has to stay on top of every aspect of the show, from set design to editing, writing, scheduling, location scouting. It's a frantic job, especially for this series, which keeps its slate filled with guest directors, a huge roster of guest stars, and a schedule that produces three episodes at a time.

"I love this show. It represents onscreen a lot of the politics that I believe in."

Rose Lam describes her day: "We're always working with three episodes on any given day. We'll have many meetings. In between the meetings, I'll check in and spend time on set with our staff, shooting crew, the cast. When you prep an episode we have kind of day one, two, three, four, five, six, seven prep, and it all spills to the last day of prep, which is usually your read-through. And by that day, you have all of your locations selected, your guest actors hopefully booked as well. Every department knows what the director and Ilene and I are trying to achieve in that episode. Episodes are on a three-week schedule: a week of prep, eight days to shoot, and four days to edit."

A Hostess of Responsibilities

"Each of our many departments has a department head: set decorator; production designer; casting; post-production, which includes editing and sound. I am responsible for the day-to-day operations of actually getting our pages of scripts filmed. I do virtually all of the editing with the editors, but the overall responsibility is mine in terms of making sure we deliver on time. All problems usually come to me."

L Is for Loving the Job

"Ilene and I have a great partnership because she's so responsive to the kind of needs that I'm faced with and I'm really responsive to her creative needs. It's a real collaboration. I love this show. It represents onscreen a lot of the politics that I believe in. I love the drama. It's a good series. Behind the scenes I love it because we've had the same crew virtually for three years. They love the show, too. We definitely push the envelope where you would think that on any given group of one hundred fifty to two hundred people they're not all going to agree with it and they don't, but they're committed enough and believe in us enough that they always open these doors and that's what it's about."

L Words: The Writing Process

Every member of the show—from the cast and directors to the hair and makeup stylists to the set designers and film editors—relies on the script. It is the glue that holds everyone together.

    The L Word writing meetings are held in the Los Angeles office. Ilene Chaiken is the head writer of the show, and there are usually five or six writers on her staff per season. By the time Ilene comes to the "room" for their first meeting, she's made a few big decisions about the upcoming season and then opens the floor to the staff and starts mapping out the stories. They lay it out on a chart and divide the season in half, working on six at a time.

Ilene Chaiken on spinning out a season full of drama: "We're always going beyond, and looking backward and forward. Every story informs every other story. Pieces move around, and we just keep adding and layering and revising until we feel we have the basic shape and at a certain point we have episode one on the board.

    "Once we have planned out what will happen with all of the characters, I will assign an episode to a writer and ask for a three-page synopsis, six episodes at a time. They describe basically what's happening, and I deliver six episodes to the network, each with a three-page synopsis on six episodes, and then I usually break it down character by character. A couple of days after I turn it in, I sit down with my Showtime

"We're always going beyond, and looking backward and forward. Every story informs every other story."

colleagues and we go through it, and they give me a few notes. For the most part, we're very thorough, and we know what we're about and they sign off on it. They give us quite a lot of freedom. I go back and convey their handful of notes to the writers, and then I assign the scripts. For example, in season two, I wrote seven of the twelve episodes and assigned the other five. I ask [writers] to turn in a very detailed outline to me. We work the outline back and forth until I feel like it's there, and then that writer goes and writes her script. I do the final edit on the script before I send it to the network. I go back and forth several times with them, sometimes with the writer, and sometimes alone."

The Art of Collaboration

Co-Executive Producer Rose Troche: It's hard to distinguish what's my creation from what's Ilene's and someone else's. For example, I had the pleasure of writing Melvin Porter first. He appeared in "Lawfully," which is an episode I wrote. Melvin is someone I understood because I come from a very religious family; my Puerto Rican family is Baptist Fundamentalist, so I grew up with that righteousness. Also, growing up first-generation American was in some ways similar to growing up in an African-American family outside of the larger community, and you think, If I act this way and this way and this way, I will get acceptance from the white community. I will be an upstanding citizen. I will make them know that not every black man carries a gun and is a felon.

I think as the show has gone on, Ilene has become a stronger and stronger writer. Characters are very well defined. I love to write for Bette; I love to write Bette's righteousness. I love to have her get angry and go off. I remember watching "L'Ennui." I don't remember who wrote it, but I was like, Oh my God, those are all of my cheesy jokes! In our meetings, we extricate and then weigh in on how much we can improve it because we're all so much a part of it. We're so in it. But Ilene is definitely the mom.

The Cooperative Effort
An Exclusive Peek into the Writers' Room

Rose Troche: We meet in the morning and snack way too much—healthy snacks. We don't do Oreos. They're organic snacks. Grapes and cheese. Nuts. If we were in New York, we'd be smoking. This is when we map out the entire season, the first half and the second half. We brainstorm. Where are our characters? What can we do? What stories are strong? We start with broad strokes. We break it down by character, and then we go into detail. Like, this year Shane's going to move in with Jenny and they're going to get a roommate that we made a videographer. All that is gone over in the room. Most of the stuff you see on the screen in one form

"We meet in the morning and snack way too much—healthy snacks. We don't do Oreos."

or another is all of those ideas. Sometimes you'll see the same idea but executed in a completely different way onscreen. Sometimes we lay out a whole story line for an actor that we can't afford; nothing happens. I'd say eighty percent is there. All of us are all over it.

Stanching Information Overflow

Rose Troche: If you ask people, they'll say everything changes after the second half of the season, and on some level it does. It changes completely. We will write the scripts, and we only get so many scripts done before the season begins. All the ones we get done are the ones that change the most because there's a domino effect. We usually put way too much stuff in each episode, and then we have to figure out what to do in the episode. The excess will flow into the next one. So the time line and the story line will change depending on that. There's too much information.

Cast Some Input

Rose Troche: Ilene will always listen to the actors. In the beginning of the season, Ilene will meet with the actors and say, Here's what we were thinking of as your general story line for the season and then sometimes she'll come back from that lunch and say let's get rid of that. *The L Word* is not a show where the writer is on set. Ilene is usually the writer and she's around, but she's not on set. You have a new director every episode, so the actors are used to taking care of their characters. None of them abuses that power.

Meet the Writers

Here are the writers whose job it is to wind us up, send our imaginations reeling, and challenge everything we thought we knew about love, family, friendship, and sex for thirteen consecutive weeks a year.

The Season One Writing Staff

Executive Producer Ilene Chaiken is a screenwriter and the author of the Golden Globe Award–winning screenplay for *Dirty Pictures*, a Showtime Original Movie. *The L Word* is her first television series.

Co-Executive Producer Ellie Herman has written for *Desperate Housewives*, *My So-Called Life*, *Chicago Hope*, *Melrose Place*, *Northern Exposure*, and *Newhart*.

Co-Executive Producer Rose Troche writes and directs for the show. Her films include the lesbian classic *Go Fish*, which she co-wrote with the show's story editor Guinevere Turner, and *Bedrooms and Hallways*, and *The Safety of Objects*, an adaptation of the story collection by season two staff writer A. M. Homes. Rose continues her dual role in seasons two and three.

Consulting Producer Mark Zakarin has written and produced the upcoming film *Lucky 13*, directed by Scott Marshall, starring Jami Gertz, Daryl Hannah, Jeremy Piven, and Garry Marshall.

Consulting Producer Susan Miller has written for the classic television series *The Paper Chase*.

Story Editor Guinevere Turner serves two roles on the show: as an actor and a writer. She appears in the show as Alice's conniving ex, Gabby Deveaux. In addition to writing *Go Fish* with Troche, she has also collaborated with filmmaker Mary Harron (who directed "Liberally") on the screenplays for *American Psycho* and the forthcoming *The Notorious Bettie Page*, and has appeared in over a dozen films to date. She returns for season two as the show's executive story editor.

Staff Writer Angela Robinson wrote and directed *D.E.B.S.* and left *The L Word* to direct *Herbie: Fully Loaded*, which starred Lindsay Lohan. She is returning to the show to direct an episode in season three.

The Season Two Writing Staff

Executive Producer Ilene Chaiken

Co-Executive Producer David Stenn wrote the television miniseries *The Secrets of Lake Success* and has written for *Beverly Hills, 90210; 21 Jump Street;* and *Hill Street Blues,* to name a few.

Co-Executive Producer Rose Troche

Producer Elizabeth Hunter has written for *ER* and *Charmed,* and wrote the screenplays for the films *The Fighting Temptations, Beauty Shop,* and the upcoming *White Boy Shuffle.*

Executive Story Editor Guinevere Turner

Staff Writer A. M. Homes is a renowned fiction writer and art critic, who has seen two of her works realized on the silver screen: *The Safety of Objects* and her debut novel, *Jack.*

Staff Writer Lara Spotts has worked as a film editor, an actress, and a senior story producer before joining *The L Word*'s writing staff.

Lights, Camera, Action:
The Filmmakers of
The L Word

Ilene Chaiken determined from the outset that *The L Word* would distinguish itself from other television series by using filmmakers to direct most episodes. The directors, many of whom have never worked in television before, are given free rein, which gives them room to experiment. But they also have a fixed script, cast, and crew, and they have a set, tight schedule in which to work: eight days of preparation, eight days of shooting, and four days of editing.

Ilene Chaiken: We've worked with fabulous film directors, some of the absolute best. I welcome directorial style and interpretation. I think that the characters are really strong, and the actresses know who they are. The scripts have continuity, and I love that different filmmakers come in and interpret them and bring their stylistic flourishes and different ideas. I never, ever said to a director, This is how we do this. It's fresh and interesting for me to let directors do their thing and let them teach me something about this show and these characters. The decision we made early on was that I wanted to work with filmmakers, that I was going to try from the very beginning to get really interesting and diverse filmmakers, people whose movies I admired, and that I didn't want to work with anybody who was a career television director. It doesn't mean I won't work with people who've directed episodes of television. Every director I've worked with has made a movie or two, and I hire them based on the movies. As I started working with them all, I realized I wasn't interested in saying, These are the conventions of the show and this is how we tell our stories. I was much more interested in inviting the directors to come in and interpret our characters and our stories.

> **"It's fresh and interesting for me to let directors do their thing and let them teach me something about this show and these characters."**

Some of *The L Word*'s Guest Directors

Tricia Brock ("Land Ahoy"): The director of the 2004 film *Killer Diller,* Brock has also worked as a television writer for such programs as *Twin Peaks, Family Law,* and *Due East.* "Land Ahoy" is filmed on an Olivia cruise, and one famous scene has Dana and Alice living out a *Love Boat* sex fantasy, dressed as Captain Steubing and Julie McCoy.

Lisa Cholodenko ("Lynch Pin"): Cholodenko burst onto the scene in 1998 with *High Art,* casting Ally Sheedy as a Nan Goldin–like photographer, followed four years later by *Laurel Canyon,* starring Frances McDormand as the pot-smoking, free-lovin' music producer mother to an uptight medical school intern played by Christian Bale. "Lynch Pin" is the episode that first introduces three crucial but very different characters: Helena Peabody, Mark Wayland, and Veronica Bloom. It also features Jenny's and Shane's memorably hilarious roommate interviews.

Ernest Dickerson ("Luminous"): A veteran cinematographer and television and film director, Dickerson has directed such movies as *Juice, Blind Faith, Bones,* and *Never Die Alone,* among others. In "Luminous," Alice and Dana announce their relationship to their friends, Jenny has a writing breakthrough, and Shane has an OxyContin-driven meltdown.

John Curran ("L'Chaim"): Curran made his big directorial debut in 2004 with the film adaptation of Andre Dubus's story collection, *We Don't Live Here Anymore,* starring Mark Ruffalo, Peter Krause, Naomi Watts, and Laura Dern, about the dark side of marriage. "L'Chaim" is the episode featuring the death of Melvin Porter, Jenny's cathartic and violent striptease at a go-go bar, and a chance encounter between Dana and Lara that will mark the end of Alice.

Tony Goldwyn ("L'Ennui"; "Limb from Limb"; "Late, Later, Latent"): An actor and a director, Goldwyn has directed *A Walk on the Moon, Someone Like You,* and the forthcoming *The Last Kiss,* but he got started directing television with *The L Word.* He also appears on the show as closeted movie star Burr Connor.

Tony Goldwyn explains the difference between directing a feature film, a network drama, and *The L Word:*

"The thing I like about television is that there are certain stories that need to be told in a television format, particularly with *The L Word.* I've worked on network shows like *Without a Trace,* and those were much more circumscribed in how they did things. There's a real style to the way Bruckheimer shows are done and they're very talented people, but that was sort of like plugging into a piece of machinery. With Ilene, every episode is different, and yet she's very fluid in the way that she writes, so every episode is a living, breathing thing until you're done, whereas most television—the script is what it is. Ilene approaches things much more the way you would a feature film. Each episode is like directing a little independent movie, with the difference being that it's really her vision that I'm trying to realize, as opposed to something that I'm independently bringing to it."

Mary Harron ("Liberally"): The director of *I Shot Andy Warhol*, Harron has collaborated with *The L Word*'s executive story editor Guinevere Turner on her two most recent films, *American Psycho* and *The Notorious Bettie Page*. In this episode Tina starts working at the Headquarters for Social Justice, and Bette first meets Candace Jewell.

Alison Maclean ("Loyal"): Maclean is perhaps best known for her second film, *Jesus' Son,* which starred Billy Crudup and Jack Black in the adaptation of the Denis Johnson novel. After enduring a season of anguish, Bette's luck starts to change in "Loyal": She shows up Helena and Leo at a CAC meeting by impressing a sought-after artist, and her friends forgo Helena's housewarming party and instead go to her door to express their solidarity.

Dan Minahan ("Lawfully"; "Life, Loss, Leaving"): Minahan cowrote *I Shot Andy Warhol* with Mary Harron. He has directed episodes of HBO's *Six Feet Under* and *Deadwood. Simply Halston,* forthcoming in 2006, is his first film. He directed the second season opener of *The L Word,* an emotionally charged episode that includes the first confrontation between a secretly pregnant Tina and a visibly distraught Bette since their breakup a month earlier; a confusing and violent parting between Jenny and Tim, who moves to Ohio; and the introduction of a new resident hottie named Carmen de la Pica Morales, who is determined to break through Shane's steely reserve.

Jeremy Podeswa ("Lagrimas de Oro"): A prolific television director who has worked on a number of series, including HBO's *Six Feet Under, Carnivàle,* and *Rome,* as well as Showtime's *Queer as Folk,* Podeswa has also written and directed the films *The Five Senses* and *Eclipse.* He directed the landmark episode depicting the first-ever lesbian sex scene featuring a pregnant woman.

Jeremy Podeswa on reworking Jenny's fantasy life in "Lagrimas de Oro":

"You get a lot of creative leeway on this show. They make a real effort to bring in people who are interesting and have very strong personal voices as filmmakers. Ilene is one of the most egoless producers I've ever worked with. She just hands things over to you and gives you freedom. She's so happy for you to bring your own stuff to the table. I was talking to Ilene about a couple scenes that I wasn't so sure about and she said, 'Well, do you want to rewrite them?' I was surprised. She said, 'If you have some good ideas, go ahead and rewrite them.' She really understands that whatever can make it better makes it better. She's a very confident person to be able to say that. I really admire that."

Kari Skogland ("Listen Up"): The writer and director of the 1996 film *The Size of Watermelons*, Skogland's episode not only introduces Jenny's best friend, Annette, but reveals another facet of Jenny's personality: her sense of humor. In this poignant episode, Annette and Jenny stalk Marina's mysterious and sophisticated girlfriend, Francesca Wolff, to assess the competition.

Burr Steers ("Labyrinth"): Steers directed the indie favorite *Igby Goes Down* (2002), which starred Jeff Goldblum, Susan Sarandon, and Rory Culkin. "Labyrinth" is a pivotal episode: Dana and Alice finally get it on in one of the sweetest, funniest sex scenes in the series, but the good feelings come crashing down at Dana and Tonya's engagement party when Alice realizes how deeply in love she is with her best friend. And Jenny and Shane's new roommate, Mark, plants hidden cameras throughout their house, including their bedrooms.

Lynne Stopkewich ("Longing"; "Locked Up"; "Lap Dance"): The filmmaker of *Kissed* and *Suspicious River*, Stopkewich has directed episodes in which Bette and Jenny have fainted, the girls have been incarcerated, and Tina gets her first lap dance. She knows how to get everyone into trouble, at least on camera.

Lynne Stopkewich talks about first meeting Ilene Chaiken and Rose Troche

"I was shooting a film in Vancouver, and Ilene and Rose came to meet me on set in my trailer. I was trying to eat lunch quickly and they just really wanted to make eye contact with me and get a sense of who I was, which doesn't happen in television that often. People look at your reel and offer you a job. There was immediately this personal touch which, for me, made the show special and continues to make the show special. I've done four episodes—two in the first season, one in the second, one in the third—and I'm always eager to come back to the show because it's really fun."

Rose Troche ("The Pilot"; "Let's Do It"; "Luck, Next Time"; "Looking Back"; "Loneliest Number"; "Loud and Proud"): Rose Troche burst onto the indie film scene in 1994 with the seminal hipster lesbian film *Go Fish.* Since then, she has made two more films: *Bedrooms and Hallways* and *The Safety of Objects,* and directed an episode of *Six Feet Under.* Rose Troche is the co-executive producer of *The L Word,* serves as a director and a writer on the show, and has been on staff since the pilot.

Clement Virgo ("Lies, Lies, Lies"; "Losing It"): The maker of such films as *Lie with Me, The Planet of Junior Brown,* and *Rude,* Virgo's episodes not only introduce Lisa, the male-identified lesbian, who becomes a temporary solution to Alice's girl problems, and Jenny's mentor Nick Barashkov, a writing professor whose past sexual history with Jenny puts Tim on edge but his are also the episodes that feature Tim's discovery of Jenny's affair with Marina and the immediate aftermath.

Los Angel-izing Vancouver:
A Conversation About Sets and Settings

The L Word is set in Los Angeles, but the show is filmed in Vancouver, British Columbia, for nearly six months out of the year (with the exception of location shots in Los Angeles, which are done in the fall for about two weeks). Production Designer Ricardo Spinacé and his team, Set Designer Linda Vipond and her team, and Director of Photography Bob Aschmann have the challenge of making a very distinctive city like Vancouver appear to be Los Angeles, using three indoor main stages filled with sets that include The Planet, the CAC, and the women's houses and apartments. They also have location scouts scouring the city in search of buildings and neighborhoods with architecture that resembles that in pockets of Los Angeles. Here, they explain the transformation on camera from Vancouver to Los Angeles, detail interior metamorphoses like the recent set makeovers of The Planet and Jenny's house, and expand on sets and sensibilities.

Ricardo, as production designer you work closely with the location scouts and you also build the sets. How do you pull off this urban masquerade act, turning a northwestern Canadian city into a Southern California urban mecca?

Ricardo Spinacé: One of the most important things is that, because of the type of city that Vancouver is, with lots of scenery around it, nature in such proximity, the skyline is very important, the architecture of the buildings, certainly, the greenery most importantly. Vancouver has a tendency to be very coniferous. LA, on the other hand, has more palms, more semiarid, so we have to really watch that. Sometimes we can have that vegetation around, but sometimes it's a matter of turning the camera a little bit so the landscape doesn't give anything away. Vancou-

"What viewers don't know is that all of the sets—the houses, The Planet—sit inside a stage area, which looks like a big warehouse."

ver also has a tendency to have a lot more redbrick construction than LA, and perhaps it's because of the history of earthquakes and masonry not standing up. LA has a tendency to have more stucco, for example. We veer away from showing brick buildings. Brick also looks more like American East Coast, like anywhere from Charleston to New York. That could be confusing visually, so we try to stay with the lighter-toned buildings. Sometimes painted brick will work. Even if I find a location where the lawn hasn't been watered, that appeals to me more for LA than a luxurious green lawn because there are a lot of water shortages in LA, a lot of restrictions—a little detail like this can matter. There are many reasons for choosing a location. Also, we spend a lot of time with graphics covering up things that give away our location in Canada, like flags and signs. For example, all of our exit signs in Canada are red, and in LA they are green, so everywhere we go, I have to change the exit sign color.

What's a good example of an LA building?

Ricardo: Marina's house in season one. Lots of concrete, hypermodern. It was a penthouse in a building and there was only one elevator. The exterior of Marina's apartment, which you see when Jenny throws the bottle of wine against the outside glass wall, was shot in LA.

What if you can't find a particular pocket of Los Angeles in Vancouver?

Ricardo: If we can't find the exact thing in Vancouver, we have to look for options. I have to go back in time to see what the most universal look is, so I can look for a location if we're not building a set. There are decisions to be made: What locations will I build? I need to plan those in my head so I can assess how much money and effort am I going to put into this, and that is determined by how much of the script relies on this location. There are a lot of decisions to be made on an hour-by-hour basis.

The director of photography is in charge of everything involving the camera and lighting, and working with the directors. And what viewers don't know is that all of the sets—the houses, The Planet—sit inside a stage area, which looks like a big warehouse. It's very dark, and they're all lined up, one next to the other. Lighting is key. It's hard to believe when you see it on film that you're not outside, or that natural California light isn't streaming in. How do you achieve that effect, Bob?

Bob Aschmann: We sort of overfocus. It helps us that we're seeing this on high definition [HD] in that regard. There are quite a number of little technical details that are factored in that are hard to explain. But it's lighting and exposure: I try to expose it as if I were on a real location, which means that if you're on a real location, you'd have a really bright exterior and really dark interiors and you'd have a really hard time leveling the set. Obviously on a stage you don't have those restrictions. From the very beginning, we designed the stages as if they were real sets. There are ceilings everywhere, and that's not traditional for stage lighting. You put your lights on the ceiling. I didn't do that. I had ceilings on everything. My goal is to make the studio look like it's a real location, bring the real world in the studio. It's a huge challenge.

Ricardo, when you build a set, you have to consider the character's personality and the needs of the crew. Can you describe a set you've built and why you made the decisions you did based on that character?

Ricardo: I'll describe Shane's room. She's the kind of person who travels light—a female James Dean. We have established a couple of things: She can paint. She painted her room this chocolate brown. We made a bed out of bare plywood. It's quite funky and uninviting since she doesn't like sleepovers. It fits together like an Ikea piece. There isn't a line of dialogue about it, explaining it, but the idea is that Shane built the bed herself.

How about transforming The Planet from Marina's café to Kit's place?

Ricardo: The Planet was up already when I began, and basically I left it as it was for the time being, except for a few things. My vision for the show is that the character of the set is there

Katherine Moennig on Her Favorite Sets:

"I love shooting scenes at Shane and Jenny's house. I always find that I'm doing scenes in the kitchen. But I'm happiest doing scenes in the living room or in Shane's bedroom. Ricardo and Linda and everyone did a really good job on the sets. Sometimes I find myself asking, Where was Shane and Jenny's house when I was looking for a home in LA? They have a big house and an outdoor shed that they converted into something else. And those girls always have new furniture. I don't know how we get it. We'll have a gray couch and then all of a sudden a green pleather couch turns up. And new dining room chairs. Where did we get this furniture? In part, I'm looking at the fictional story, wondering when we found these new chairs, but I admit that it's also because I've been on a quest for new dining room chairs for the last few months and I still can't find the perfect set."

when it needs to be in terms of texture, but otherwise I like a rather clean, modern, uncluttered look. In that regard I am very close to Bob Aschmann. That's why I'm so happy with this, because Bob and I really connect very well, and that's very important. As long as he likes what I do for his camera, then everything is great and great things happen. I built new tables, which are triangular in shape because it's much more camera-friendly.

Linda, as the set designer, you also participated in The Planet's makeover. What kind of flourishes say this is now Kit's place?

Linda Vipond: To reflect Kit's personality, which is much warmer, much friendlier, it needs to look like a welcoming, comfortable place. It began as a coffee shop and it has just kept evolving from the beginning. Now it has quite high-end food and a new food-prep bar. It has a chef and another bar in there to serve alcohol. It was really interesting for me because you don't often get a chance, especially in this business, to do something a second time. And we found 1950s bar chairs, stripped them and had them painted with automotive paint, and re-covered them. I love them. We're still changing it. We just put a new mural in there and new curtains, so it's a constantly evolving process, which is what I really like creatively. It's fabulous.

One of your challenges is picking out the furniture and the art for the sets. On this cast, we have Bette, who is a curator and collector, and we also have characters who span the economical range from postcollegiate broke to a comfortable six figures. How do

you convey that on the sets without some sets looking too stark and others looking too opulent?

Linda: Tim's and Jenny's house, which then became Jenny's and Shane's, was quite a difficult thing because they don't have money to go out and buy stuff. So who are they and how do you reflect that in the decoration? For filming, you can't have a bare house, so you have to have art on the walls, and furniture, and you also want to say something about that character. So in meetings with Ilene and Rose Troche, we decided that, for example, Shane made her own bed and did the painting on her walls. There's only one piece of art above her bed, and we discussed that for ages and ages until we finally decided on a Man Ray print. And then we were going around about which Man Ray. We were shooting it the next day, and I just picked a 1931 untitled photo and said this is the one, because you can just make yourself completely nuts.

When we moved Jenny in from the studio apartment into the house from season one to two, that was a big change for her. She was going through a lot of difficult things to find herself, and we wanted to reflect that in the decoration of the room. And that's why there was a circus theme, which reflected her fantasies and her writing. There was [an] underlying family historical theme to do with her Jewish heritage and things that had transpired in her youth. And we wanted to marry the idea of what she was going through to the flashback, so we brought in a lot of circus-related iconography. Mia also [had] a lot of ideas.

Bette's and Tina's house is kind of midcentury modern. When we did the first season, Ilene really had a definite idea about who Bette is. Bette is wearing the pants in that family, so to speak. Ilene gave us really clear guidelines: no patterns, clean lines, no clutter. She gave us details about what type of artwork Bette would like. We didn't have enough money starting out. So when I bought that stuff three years ago, a lot of that stuff was just before it was popular. The chairs in their living room I bought at a thrift store for thirty dollars—you can look in a design magazine and it's almost the same frame. So I just hit that mark. It was just a timing thing because if I did it now, they would probably be gone. I got everything reupholstered. That was the only way that I could do that house because it's so costly and we were setting up The Planet, Shane's, Bette's and Tina's, apartments for Alice, Dana, and Kit that first year. We did that in six weeks. We have a great team here. I have great buyers; it's really a team thing. You can't do this on your own.

Locking It In
Editing and
Post-production:

A conversation with film editors Lisa Robison and Lisa Binkley and post-production supervisor Louisa Rees

Once the directors have finished their weeklong shoots, they turn everything over to editing and post-production. Award-winning film editors Lisa Robison and Lisa Binkley—a couple who have been together for ten years—explain how they can help a director transform twenty-four hours of raw footage into a beautiful and engaging hour-long narrative. Post-production supervisor Louisa Rees, who oversees the editors and coordinates sound and quality control among other things, makes sure we can hear and see everything.

What do you do from day to day?

Lisa Robison, film editor: I've worked on the show since the pilot, and before that I worked on feature films and television series. Our days here are long. It's picking and choosing and cutting it down. Three hours of footage from one day of shooting, and the show is only an hour long. And we shoot for eight days. That can mean twenty-four hours of footage pared down to a one-hour show.

Lisa Binkley, film editor: I joined the show on the second season. There is one thing about editing that people don't understand. It's not just about picking out all of the good stuff. It's a little more involved than that. It's your analysis of the footage. The trick is, when you're editing, you're storytelling for the second time. The first time it's told through the script because it's written in the story. Then the director comes and retells that script as another secondary story. Then the third time you get that story is in the editing room when you're analyzing the performances and what you're given. It's your job to put together in an eloquent way that will get the story across in a strong way. So you're selecting.

Louisa Rees, post-production supervisor: The turnaround is fast. The directors who come in are feature film directors and they want that kind of creative input, but realistically speaking, they have eight days to shoot it, which means that the editors have eight days to assemble it. Then a director comes in for four days and then it moves along in that production. It goes to producer cut, down to the network, back again, and then we lock it. It's a long haul for the amount of footage we get in eight days. I oversee everything that goes all the way from editing to mixing and delivering the show: sound, vision. Because we have three editors who do a rotation, I have to know every show from start to finish, which can be overwhelming at times because, even though each one is independently shot like a feature film, it still runs like a TV series. It's all very fast paced and demanding. It's also a heavy, heavy music show, too. During the prep, we end up having a music meeting with the director and editor and Ilene and [composer] Elizabeth Ziff. When the editors are giving their cut, they put temporary music in and then the director comes in and has ideas and puts more music in.

How strictly must you follow the script? Do you have a bit of creative leeway?

Lisa Binkley: We follow the scripts, but we can change it as well. It's written in a certain order, and then when you're reviewing your footage, and you're putting your scenes together as days are getting along, you might realize, this scene doesn't work logically. Technically you're supposed to make your editor's cut follow exactly what's written, but on this show they trust us to make adjustments.

Lisa Robison: It's an editor's job to think outside the box. We get a lot of creative freedom. We've never had so much as we've had on this show. The wackiest thing I did: In the opening of the pilot, I feel like I totally changed it with jump cuts. I used Marianne Faithfull's "Pleasure Song." Bette and Tina are waking up and Tim is preparing the house. That took a long time. It was differently written on the page than edited.

What is it like to work with a different film director every episode?

Lisa Binkley: The directors come in for four days to review the edit. They're used to having months. They are aware of every little detail. They are intense. It's the director's vision. From an editor's standpoint, the editor is the one person who is analyzing footage from the very beginning before it is even cut. And so while you're working, you're seeing different versions of the same thing. You're

> # "That can mean twenty-four hours of footage pared down to a one-hour show."

"Editors are often referred to as ghosts because we make things happen but nobody sees us."

telling the same story, but a different way of looking at it. So your job as the editor, too, is to file things away, to recall the ideas that have been put out there, and when the producer comes in and says a scene isn't working, as an editor you can address it because it's been changed. You have to maintain what the director ultimately wants and what the producer wants and take those two ideas and get what makes everybody happy because you work the material over so many times. You're an interpreter in a way.

What is the strangest aspect of your job?

Lisa Binkley: We are staring at these people, and these actors' performances all the time. It's what's so weird about editing. For hours and hours. You analyze their every move. You're with them all day long, you know them so well.

Lisa Robison: Editors are often referred to as ghosts because we make things happen but nobody sees us.

Louisa: Except here, because we're all in one place.

Lisa Robison: Yeah, and we're doing our best to make them look good.

Lisa Binkley: We can even manipulate a performance, a moment. Improve it.

What happens once the director is satisfied with the edit?

Louisa: When everyone is satisfied, you lock it. We do a music slot and a sound slot. When we start doing this it's pretty much dry. Elizabeth Ziff will listen to everything that's been sourced in there. She'll decide if it stays or if she's going to score something. That's one whole session. And then we do a dialogue spot. The show is so dialogue-driven that we have our sound facility do a tech spot for us to detect how clear and audible everything is. We usually do an additional dialogue recording—ADR. I have to get the actors back into the sound studio to rerecord their lines. It's usually about one hundred seventy-five lines each episode. We do this so we can hear their lines more clearly. Then we go to color correcting, titling, laying back music, shipping, quality check, and then, after all that, we finally send it off to the network.

Laying Down the Tracks
The Music of *The L Word*

A conversation with Elizabeth Ziff, composer and founding member of BETTY

Elizabeth Ziff joined *The L Word* on the second season as the composer. She works with music supervisor Natasha Duprey to select and cue in all the music for each episode. But her unique position at the show involves several other roles: With her band, BETTY, she has written and performed the show's new theme song, "The Way That We Live." She has composed an original score for the show. And with Carmen as a master DJ and the transformation of The Planet into Kit's dream music venue, well, let's just say Ziff has her work cut out for her. Here is how she makes the music play.

How did BETTY get invited to write the theme song?

Elizabeth Ziff: The writing of the theme song was a total adjunct to being hired as the composer. Ilene came to see our play, *BETTY Rules!* She hosted a benefit for breast cancer research that we did in Chicago, and she loved it. She loved the music, loved everything about it. Showtime decided that they wanted a new theme song, and they asked a few people to submit. They liked ours the best. One of the reasons BETTY was asked to submit a song was because of our history: We have been plugging away for Pro-Choice, AIDS, gay rights. And we've also done a lot of television. [BETTY produced the theme song for the HBO series *Real Sex,* as well as songs for Lifetime, Nickelodeon, and national commercials. They've also appeared in films and on film soundtracks such as *The*

The L Word Theme Song: "The Way That We Live"

*Girls in tight dresses who drag with
    mustaches
chicks driving fast
ingénues with long lashes
women who long, love, lust
women who give
This is the way
it's the way that we live
Talking laughing loving breathing
    fighting fucking crying drinking
    writing winning losing cheating
    kissing thinking dreaming
This is the way,
it's the way that we live
It's the way that we live, and love.*

Written, performed and produced by BETTY
Lyrics and music by BETTY copyright © 2005

Out-of-Towners, Life with Mikey, It's Pat, and *The Incredibly True Adventures of Two Girls in Love.*] We worked closely with Ilene on it, went back and forth on it a few times, and we all really, really liked it. Ilene thought it really represented the show because it's fun and upbeat, and sort of drum and bass. And she wanted it to be overtly sexual. There was an initial flip-out with the new theme song. People were asking, "What the fuck is this?" But by the end of the season, when BETTY were traveling and we'd start to play the song, people would go nuts. We sold a lot of copies of the score, too, which is great. The viewers really pay attention to all the music.

What is it like adding this whole new live-music dimension to the show?

It was one of the things they brought me in for: the reality aspect of it. I've been doing music for so long, playing in clubs and booking clubs. When you watch the live music on the show, a lot of people don't know that everyone is lip-synching, but all of the equipment is real, all plugged in.

You also have the job of coming up with playlists for DJ Carmen de la Pica Morales.

I've been playing music for twenty years, so I have really, really diverse taste. I was a DJ once, a long time ago—not like we have DJs now. But in "Life, Loss, Leaving" there's a scene where Carmen and Shane are about to fuck in a studio. Carmen played something for Shane and says that mix was where she wanted to be in five years. That was my remix of the theme song.

What do you see as your mandate when choosing the soundtrack for the show?

I like to give props to people who have been in the gay and lesbian music scene for years, and have given to the community, and I want the music that we have on the show to reflect the diversity of the community. The last song in the season two finale was Sweet Honey in the Rock singing a Ferron song. We put a lot of thought into the music. We want great music to not only help the story along lyrically and musically but also to give [a] history of the community. That's one of the reasons I'm here, to bring that history in, because I've been a part of that history and of that community for the past twenty years.

The music in the first season was good, but it wasn't as memorable as it should have been. Our community is so music-oriented. Music is

> # "When you watch the live music on the show, a lot of people don't know that everyone is lip-synching."